# A Parade
# of Puppet Plays

# A Parade of Puppet Plays

Abingdon Press
Nashville

# A Parade of Puppet Plays

0-687-02666-0

03  04  05  06  07  08  09  10  11  12 — 10  9  8  7  6  5  4  3  2  1

Manufactured in the United States of America

# Acknowledgments

There cannot be puppet plays without puppeteers and an audience. The puppeteers give life to the puppets, and the audience gives us a reason for existence. Therefore I wish to acknowledge those who have been crucial in the initial performance of these plays:

The people of Forest Street United Methodist Church – Clarksville, Tennessee
Mitch Truesdale aka Grandpa
Mitchell Truesdale aka Grumpy and/or Tee
Beverly Head aka Mrs. Munk
Rhonda Wolfe aka Mrs. Bea
and all those who stepped in as substitutes.

# Dedication

To the young folks and the older folks who haven't forgotten what it was like to be young. Especially to the children at Forest Street United Methodist Church.

To my sister Elizabeth Harrub Epps, who shipped a box full of puppets, anticipating that they might come to life in my worship setting.

To my wife, Nancy, who is my harshest critic, my best fan, and the person who displayed extraordinary patience as we worked through the editing.

And, of course, to the honor and glory of God.

# Contents

The plays are in order to follow the calendar year.
Feel free to start in mid-year, using the introductory plays
and altering the sequence to correspond with holidays or events.

# Introduction

Hi there! This would be a lot easier if we could just sit down together and talk about puppets. Since we can't do that, I am compelled to write a few helpful hints for those who have enough courage and enough faith to use puppets as one more way to communicate the Gospel.

These plays target children who are about ages four to twelve. The Forest Street Puppeteers have been delighted to discover that the adults in our congregation enjoy the presentations as much as the children. Each play begins with an introductory statement by a leader (or pastor). The introduction attempts to tie the current play to previous plays and build some continuity. Our puppeteers almost always end the play with an echo prayer; one of the characters will say a phrase, and the children repeat the phrase. If you choose to do the prayer in this way, break it up into phrases before giving it to the character who will be leading the prayer.

You have permission to photocopy these plays for use in your church. Photocopy one for each character and attach the copies to the staging in front of the puppeteers. The puppeteers will do a better job if they practice a couple of times to get the movements and the words coordinated; and they'll find it easier if they use a highlighter marker on the lines for their characters.

Our puppet community consists of about two dozen human type and animal characters. You don't need that many. These plays are limited to Grandpa, Reverend Puggins, Grumpy, Mrs. Bea, Mrs. Munk, Mr. Ratchet, and Tee. Those seven, with perhaps a visit by a sock puppet, can perform the entire series. On the next two pages you'll find a brief character description of each puppet.

Experienced puppeteers don't need this word of advice, but for beginners it is crucial! The advice is: Relax! The more you enjoy the production, the more your audience will respond. Feel free to ad lib when the need arises or when current events dictate a subject that needs attention. Our puppets have introduced guest speakers, given a report at our annual Charge Conference, and discussed budget issues. We find that they can touch delicate issues in non-threatening ways, sometimes bringing humor to tough situations.

Our stage is PVC piping with a wonderful starry curtain all around. It is high enough for the puppeteers to sit comfortably behind it. It is portable and collapsible. It tends to disappear on Communion Sundays. Hinged plywood would also work very well. Several puppet stages are included in the back of the book.

All that being said, you still might have reservations or questions. I can be reached by e-mail at Bud1941@vol.com. We've had a good experience at Forest Street. I'd like to help you have the same.

And now let me introduce you to the cast.

Harmony is the kind of place where we'd all like to live. I think it is somewhere nearby, just over the horizon. I suppose Harmony can be anywhere. The people who live in Harmony are ordinary types who have both strengths and weaknesses. As our puppets developed character, here is what we have discovered about them:

**Reverend Puggins.** He is the backbone of the spiritual community, but maybe not the wisest of the bunch. He has a great deal of education and knows his Bible—a good pastor who will often pull out biblical examples when others visit with problems. Rev. Puggins is middle-aged and given to napping and is sometimes caught mid-snore.

**Grandpa.** Here is a combination of wisdom and experience. His faith is well founded and solid. Grandpa has all the traits of a good leader, until his patience is tried by bureaucracy or his grandson, Tee. He and Tee try out retirement, and Grandpa decides that he needs to move back to Harmony. Grandpa is in his late seventies.

**Tee.** We aren't sure yet how or why Tee is in Grandpa's care. This much we do know: Tee has a funny haircut. He is impetuous and sometimes irresponsible. Tee is willing to express anger and blame others, and he has questions about faith. But all in all, Tee is a good boy. Tee is probably a ten- to twelve-year-old.

**Mrs. Munk.** She matches Grandpa in wisdom, experience, and faith. She is a very solid citizen and often is found evaluating situations and giving advice. She has children who are referred to as "the Munksters" and is a single mom. Mrs. Munk is about 30 something.

**Grumpy.** This is the fellow who gets his kicks chasing kids out of his yard and punctuating his sentences with a menacing, "Harumph!" He helped build an addition on Mrs. Munk's house, and they became close friends. Sometimes a cynic, sometimes a skeptic, sometimes compassionate, and sometimes abrasive, he is always grumpy.

**Mrs. Bea.** She arrived in Harmony after a disaster destroyed her home in a town nearby. She arrived angry at what happened and angry at God. Mrs. Bea dances around the periphery of church and faith. She is interested, but sometimes it is a self-indulgent interest. She asks for information, but often receives it on the most simplistic level. She is probably the biggest critic of everything that smells like faith, including Rev. Puggins. She is the eternal doubter, never gets quite to the point of committing herself to a life of faith.

**Mr. Ratchet.** He is nicknamed Mr. Racket because he is always making noise. It is usually a happy noise, whistling or singing. Mr. Racket is a happy fellow who shares God's love with everyone.

# GRANDPA INTRODUCES MRS. BEA AND REV. PUGGINS

### Characters:
Grandpa
Mrs. Bea
Rev. Puggins


**LEADER:** Boys and girls, we have a special guest this morning. He is a bit older than any of you. I think you'll like him. His name is Grandpa.

(*GRANDPA comes up invisible stairs to the stage.*)

**GRANDPA:** Well, hi there!

(*GRANDPA pauses for the children to respond.*)

**GRANDPA:** Now that wasn't much of a response! Maybe you could say, "Hi there, Grandpa!"

(*GRANDPA pauses again for the children to respond.*)

**GRANDPA:** That's better. I'm hoping we can be good friends. And when you come to Harmony for a little visit, I'll be around there somewhere. I've got a farm on the outskirts of town. Today I'd like to tell you about a couple of my neighbors. You'll find them in Harmony too.

GRANDPA: The first person I'd like to introduce is one of my friends in Harmony. She came to this town after her home was destroyed in a town about twenty miles away. Her name is Mrs. Bea. You never see her without her apron. She's a great cook. And if you say, "Hi, Mrs. Bea!" she might just join us.

(*GRANDPA pauses for the children to respond. MRS. BEA comes on stage.*)

MRS. BEA: Hi, Grandpa! Hi, boys and girls! If I had a big hat instead of this apron, I'd do a Minnie Pearl imitation and say, "Howdy, I'm mighty proud to be here!" I had to leave my biscuits in the oven, but I just wanted to come by and say to our new friends, "Welcome to Harmony!"

GRANDPA: Thanks for coming by, Mrs. Bea. Did you see Rev. Puggins on your way over here?

MRS. BEA: As a matter of fact, I did see him. He was napping under that big tree out front. I gave him a little kick as I walked by. Then I ducked behind the tree as he woke up. I think he was right behind me when I came in.

(*REV. PUGGINS comes up to stage stretching and yawning.*)

REV. PUGGINS: Oh, hello there. (*Yawns again*) I think a limb must have fallen from that tree out front. Something hit my leg. I was er . . . er . . . in deep meditation when it happened. It's strange, though, I didn't see any limbs on the ground.

(*REV. PUGGINS turns to MRS. BEA.*)

REV. PUGGINS: Oh hello, Mrs. Bea. It's always good to see you.

MRS. BEA: (*A bit sarcastically*) And it's always good to see you . . . with your eyes open.

GRANDPA: I was just introducing the two of you to this fine group of girls and boys. I hoped it might be a week or two before they found out too much about any of us.

MRS. BEA: Why, whatever could you be talking about, Grandpa? We are always so sweet.

GRANDPA: Ummm, well, okay. But it might not hurt to have our new friends pray for Harmony. Would you do that, kids?

**Have Grandpa pray this prayer with the children:**
Dear God, we pray for harmony and we give you thanks when we find harmony. Bless all the folks who try to live in harmony. Amen.

# GRUMPY, TEE, AND MRS. MUNK SHOW UP

## Characters:
Grumpy
Mrs. Munk
Tee

**LEADER:** Last week we met Grandpa, Rev. Puggins, and Mrs. Bea. Today we will meet some of the other characters who make up the community called Harmony.

(*GRUMPY comes upstairs to the stage. He looks all around silently.*)

**GRUMPY:** Hmmm. *Harumph!* Some of the people in Harmony call me Grumpy! What do they know? If they think I've been grumpy in the past, they haven't seen anything!

(*GRUMPY leans out toward the audience.*)

**GRUMPY:** Do I seem grumpy to you? No? I don't think so, either. So what's all the big deal? It's like they —

(*MRS MUNK interrupts GRUMPY.*)

| MRS. MUNK: | Oh, hi there, Grumpy. I bet the boys and girls already love you. Loving you is like hugging a cactus, Grumpy. When are you going to let us come close? I know that deep inside there's a kind man waiting to get out. |
|---|---|
| GRUMPY: | *Harumph!* You just keep your distance! What you see here is what you get. I'm not going to candy-coat who I am, I'm just grumpy. |
| MRS. MUNK: | You sure are. I can see that we aren't going far with this talk, but maybe I can bring Tee up for an introduction. |

(*MRS. MUNK disappears.*)

| GRUMPY: | *Harumph!* Oh no, not Tee, the brat! Not Tee, the useless kid who just had to come to Harmony and live with Grandpa! Not Tee, with that preteen hairdo and all those wacky ideas about fashions. |
|---|---|

(*MRS. MUNK and TEE come upstairs to the stage.*)

| TEE: | Hey, wow! Hi, kids! My name is Tee. Grumpy calls me Tee-bone sometimes, but it's really Tee. I think I'm about your age. I moved to Harmony, oh, about a year ago. Grandpa takes pretty good care of me. He is my real grandpa. Everybody in Harmony calls him Grandpa. I guess they do that because he's old. But he's my real grandpa. |
|---|---|
| GRUMPY: | *Harumph!* Isn't that about enough, Tee-bone? |
| TEE: | I wish you wouldn't call me that, Grumpy. |

GRUMPY: You might as well — *Harumph!* — wish for a million dollars!

TEE: Well, now that we've embarrassed ourselves, maybe we should say something good to our new friends.

GRUMPY: *Harumph!* Don't lick a flagpole in freezing weather. How's that?

MRS. MUNK: Not exactly what I had in mind. Tee, any words for our new friends?

TEE: I guess I'd just say that I look forward to seeing all of you in Harmony.

MRS. MUNK: That's better. I was hoping you'd say something about faith and love and . . . maybe I could say it in a prayer, if our new friends will help.

**Have Mrs. Munk pray this prayer with the children:**
Dear God, help us find faith and love. Help us live together in harmony. Amen.

# MRS. BEA ASKS, "HOW DO I GET JESUS INTO MY HEART?"

### Characters:
Mrs. Bea
Rev. Puggins

**LEADER:** The brotherhood parade was now just a memory, and Mrs. Bea understood what it was all about. But on the next Sunday, Rev. Puggins told the congregation that each one of them needed to have Jesus in their heart. Mrs. Bea was a little confused by that.

**MRS. BEA:** Yoo hoo . . . Rev. Puggins . . . Oh, Rev. Puggins, could I talk with you for a moment.

(*REV. PUGGINS wakes up from a nap.*)

**REV. PUGGINS:** Ummm . . . oh . . . why, hello, Mrs. Bea. What can I do for you?

**MRS. BEA:** Well, it's something you said in the sermon —

**REV. PUGGINS:** I'm delighted you were listening. Now, what was it?

| | |
|---|---|
| MRS. BEA: | I think I heard you say that we need to have Jesus in our hearts. I'm not sure how I do that. Does it take heart surgery? |
| REV. PUGGINS: | Hmmm . . . Let's see, how do I explain this? When I said heart, I really meant that Jesus should be inside of us . . . that his presence in our lives should help us make decisions every day. I was talking . . . well, not so much in literal terms — |
| MRS. BEA: | Then I won't need heart surgery? |
| REV. PUGGINS: | Nope. And with your vegetarian diet, all those salads you eat, I bet you'll never need heart surgery. |
| MRS. BEA: | But how do I get Jesus' presence into my life? I guess that's the real question. |
| REV. PUGGINS: | And that is terribly easy, and it is also terribly hard. |
| MRS. BEA: | Now you are really confusing me. I just want a straight answer . . . please. |
| REV. PUGGINS: | Well. Let me try. It is terribly easy to invite Jesus into your heart, or into your life. You simply say something like, "Lord Jesus, I'd like for you to take over my life." Now, that part is easy. What is terribly hard is allowing Jesus to gain control of our thoughts and actions. So it really is terribly easy and terribly hard. |
| MRS. BEA: | I think I understand. It's more than just asking him in, isn't it? |

REV. PUGGINS:  Oh yes! That is only the beginning. But it is a beginning. Are you going to invite him into your life, Mrs. Bea?

MRS. BEA:  Umm . . . uh . . . I've been thinking about it, but I don't think I'll do that today. Maybe next week. I wouldn't want to rush into anything.

REV. PUGGINS:  I'm sure you wouldn't, Mrs. Bea. And God will give you all the freedom you need to make such an important decision. Would you like for the boys and girls to ask God's help while you decide?

MRS. BEA:  Ohhh . . . well, I guess so.

REV. PUGGINS:  Okay, boys and girls?


**Have Rev. Puggins pray this prayer with the children:**
Dear God, there are folks here today who need to decide to put you first. Or maybe to invite you in. Give us the courage and the faith to have Jesus in our lives. Amen.

# MRS. BEA ASKS ABOUT THE WORD MADE FLESH

## Characters:
Mrs. Bea
Rev. Puggins

**LEADER:** Rev. Puggins had preached a pretty good sermon. Some folks thought it was too long, and Rev. Puggins noticed one fellow looking at his wristwatch, then shaking it to be sure it was running. But it was a good sermon. It was about God's Word and the Word made flesh. Somewhere in the midst of the sermon, Mrs. Bea got a bit confused. She caught Rev. Puggins right after the service.

**MRS. BEA:** Oh, excuse me, Rev. Puggins. I know I'm new in the community, and I haven't joined your church yet . . . but I've just got to ask you a question.

**REV. PUGGINS:** An honest question is a beautiful thing, Mrs. Bea. And it doesn't really matter that you are not a member. I do hope you'll join our church family someday, but for today I'm happy to try to answer your question. Now, what's bothering you?

MRS. BEA:    It's this. A few minutes ago you were talking about the Word, like in the Bible. And then you came along and talked about the Word made flesh . . . and that is Jesus. But which one is God's Word?

REV. PUGGINS:    Before I answer, let me say that you are asking a very good question. Lots of folks have wondered about this, but not many have asked the question. So maybe other folks will learn, and maybe our young friends will learn too! How about it, kids? Will you remember what I tell you?

(*Encourage the children to nod their heads.*)

REV. PUGGINS:    Okay, here is how it goes. In the old days — Old Testament days — the word was usually the way God spoke to us. God would speak, and let's say a prophet would hear. So the Bible would say, "The word of the Lord came to Jonah" or one of the others. Then those old guys would turn around and say, "Hear the word of the Lord."

MRS. BEA:    So God was being revealed in the word he was speaking through the people of that day.

REV. PUGGINS:    Exactly right! Then, hundreds of years later, the word was made flesh . . . God was revealed more fully in Jesus. And Jesus, as the expression — the word — and that word brings not only a better picture of God, but also a promise of life!

MRS. BEA:    But I have also heard the whole Bible called God's Word. How does that fit in?

**REV. PUGGINS:** And that is right too. It is God's Word. It is the work of inspired people who wrote down the way God was being revealed through the ages. So if you look within the Bible, which we call God's Word, you will find people proclaiming things like, "Hear the word of the Lord." And you will also find Jesus as a living word . . . And through these three, you can get a pretty good picture of God.

**MRS. BEA:** I think I've got it now. Do you kids understand? I think what it means is that God is trying to show God's self to us in lots of ways. But I guess we need to read the Bible, don't we?

**REV. PUGGINS:** Now you have really discovered something important! Jesus said, "Let anyone who has ears, hear." Today, it's more like, "Let those who wish to know God, read the Word." Now I'd like to offer a little prayer. Will you folks pray with me?

**Have Rev. Puggins pray this prayer with the children:**
Dear God, we give you thanks for the people who wrote our Bible, for words, which can change life, and for the Word, the man we call Jesus. Amen.

# GRANDPA HAS A WEE BIT OF TROUBLE

### Characters:
Grumpy
Grandpa


**LEADER:** Mrs. Bea spread a rumor last week about Tee starting a fire in the church. But it was just a rumor. And maybe Mrs. Bea learned a lesson this time. But when Grumpy met up with Grandpa, he heard about a real fire.

**GRUMPY:** Oh, hi, Grandpa! Haven't — *Harumph!* — seen you in a long time.

**GRANDPA:** Yep . . . I've been missing your *harumphs*, Grumpy.

**GRUMPY:** Grandpa, I heard —

(*GRANDPA interrupts GRUMPY.*)

**GRANDPA:** It's true, Grumpy I had a barn fire last Wednesday.

**GRUMPY:** Well, just a barn fire, that's not so bad.

| GRANDPA: | Well, it destroyed all my hay, most of my hand tools, two tractors, a combine, a hay rake, and about a ton of feed. That fire just about put me out of the farming business. And I've got to have something for my livestock. |
|---|---|
| GRUMPY: | Oh — *Harumph!* — wow! I thought a barn fire just burned up an old — *Harumph!* — empty building. But — *Harumph!* — gosh, that really must hurt. |
| GRANDPA: | Sure it hurts, Grumpy. I'm glad there weren't any injuries. You know, sometimes Tee plays in the loft. And sometimes the cattle are in the barn. I can start over on a barn, but sometimes it's hard to get over an injury or a death. |
| GRUMPY: | But you — *Harumph!* — seem so calm about this whole thing. Why I'd be fussing — *Harumph!* — for weeks. |
| GRANDPA: | Being upset wouldn't change anything, Grumpy. In fact, it might keep me from getting my barn rebuilt, Grumpy. |
| GRUMPY: | Why, Grandpa? |
| GRANDPA: | Grumpy, I have discovered that no matter what happens, it really doesn't change God's love for you, or your friend's love. And if you have those two things, it's easy to start over. |
| GRUMPY: | But Grandpa, aren't you a little . . . uh — *Harumph!* — old to start over? |

GRANDPA: Nobody is too old to start over, Grumpy. Why, just today I read about a man who just started to school to be a preacher.

GRUMPY: Lots of folks do that, Grandpa.

GRANDPA: This man was ninety-two years old, Grumpy. He figured that God wasn't through with him! I don't think he's through with me, either. I'll just rebuild my barn.

GRUMPY: Wow — *Harumph!* — Great. I'll help out! And now could we have a prayer for starting over? Kids, will you help?

**Have Grumpy pray this prayer with the children:**
Dear God, we'd like you to bless everyone who has the courage to start over. Be with our friends of all ages. Amen.

# GRANDPA VISITS REV. PUGGINS

## Characters:
Grandpa
Rev. Puggins

**LEADER:** A couple of weeks ago Grumpy heard that Grandpa's barn had burned. He didn't think it was much of a loss until Grandpa explained what was in that barn and that a fire like that could put him out of the farming business. Today, Grandpa has found Rev. Puggins . . . and Grandpa looks troubled.

**GRANDPA:** Hi, Rev. Puggins, thanks for seeing me on such short notice.

**REV. PUGGINS:** No problem, Grandpa! I always have time for you.

**GRANDPA:** I've come to see you about something serious, Rev. Puggins.

**REV. PUGGINS:** Oh . . . yes, I heard about your fire.

**GRANDPA:** Nope, that's not it at all. Well, in a way it is. You see, I've been dealing with folks a thousand miles away who have my barn insured.

**REV. PUGGINS:** Uh huh . . . go on.

**GRANDPA:** It looks like my old barn wasn't worth much. These folks who have never seen my barn or my tractors decided they were about worn out. I might not even get enough money to rebuild, and I sure won't be able to buy tractors. And, well, dealing with those folks just makes me — well, angry! Mad enough to bite nails!

**REV. PUGGINS:** So you came to me for . . . ?

**GRANDPA:** I guess I came by to see if you could help me with my anger. I don't like being angry. It sort of eats at me from the inside. You know what I mean? My world gets messed up when I carry around a load of anger. What can I do, Rev. Puggins?

**REV. PUGGINS:** In the Sermon on the Mount, Jesus tells us to "pray for those who despitefully use us." That is the best bit of advice I can give. Oh, there is one other thing . . .

**GRANDPA:** What's that?

**REV. PUGGINS:** You have a contract with the insurance company. If you don't think they are treating you right, you could hire a lawyer. That way you won't need to feel like they are taking advantage of you. Just because you are a Christian, you don't have to give in, or give up, when you are right! You can pray for those folks and still try to get what is fair.

GRANDPA: Now that is good advice! I'll start praying for those people this very day. And I'll contact my attorney in the morning. I do appreciate your advice. I couldn't see anything but anger for a week or so. I think I can get over it now.

REV. PUGGINS: We all get angry, sometimes with very good reason. Even these kids get angry. So let's pray a prayer about anger . . . okay?

**Have Rev. Puggins pray this prayer with the children:**
Dear God, please love me when I'm angry and help me to pray for the people I get angry with. Fill my heart with love and forgiveness. Amen.

# MRS. BEA WANTS TO KNOW WHY GOD LOVES US

### Characters:
Mrs. Bea
Rev. Puggins

| | |
|---|---|
| LEADER: | Mrs. Bea was still trying to get Jesus into her heart, as Rev. Puggins suggested in his sermon a couple of weeks ago. She thought she was on the right track, and she was glad it wasn't going to involve heart surgery. But then Rev. Puggins threw her a curve. He said, in his next sermon, "God loves you . . . just like you are!" |
| MRS. BEA: | Ummm, er . . . I say there, Rev. Puggins. Oh, Rev. Puggins! |
| REV. PUGGINS: | Oh, uh, yes . . . Hello, Mrs. Bea. |
| MRS. BEA: | I have a little question for you, Rev. Puggins. Just a small one. |
| REV. PUGGINS: | Sometimes small questions are the toughest, but I'll give it a try. What is your question, Mrs. Bea? |
| MRS. BEA: | You said in your sermon that God loves us, right? |
| REV. PUGGINS: | Well, yes . . . Sure! |

MRS. BEA:        Why?

REV. PUGGINS:    Why, what?

MRS. BEA:        Why does God love us?

REV. PUGGINS:    Oh, I see. Well now, let me think about my answer.

(REV. PUGGINS paces back and forth, thinking.)

REV. PUGGINS:    Ummm . . . ummm . . .

MRS. BEA:        I can hear the gears turning, but I think the transmission is slipping.

REV. PUGGINS:    I was just searching for the right words. I think I have them now.

MRS. BEA:        And?

REV. PUGGINS:    God loves us because God wants to love us!

MRS. BEA:        Not because we act nice or do good things for other folks?

REV. PUGGINS:    Nope . . . just because God wants to!

MRS. BEA:        Even when we are bad?

REV. PUGGINS:    Yep. God loves us even when we are bad!

MRS. BEA:        Now that's a hoot! You mean I could do something really, really mean, and God would still love me?

REV. PUGGINS:  Absolutely. But as soon as you realize that God loves you, you just stop wanting to do mean stuff. You want to be more like our Father . . . God.

MRS. BEA:  Even before I loved God, God loved me?

REV. PUGGINS:  Even before you were born, God loved you, just because God wanted to!

MRS. BEA:  Is there some way I can remember this? It seems really important.

REV. PUGGINS:  Sure. I'm sure the kids can help us. Instead of a prayer, kids, let's teach Mrs. Bea John 3:16 — "For God so loved the world that he gave his only Son, so that everyone who believes in him may not perish, but may have eternal life." Now you say it, Mrs. Bea.

MRS. BEA:  "For God so loved the world that he gave his only Son, so that everyone who believes in him may not perish, but may have eternal life."

# IF GOD LOVES ME, WHY DID I GET SICK?

### Characters:
Mrs. Bea
Mrs. Munk

**LEADER:** Last week, Mrs. Bea questioned Rev. Puggins about the reason God loves us. After giving the question some thought, Rev. Puggins told Mrs. Bea that God loves us because God wants to love us. God's love is not based on our being good or on our doing good things. That was hard for Mrs. Bea to understand, but she finally seemed to figure it out. On Tuesday, she attended the Harmony Mardi Gras party . . . and, well, let's see what happened. ·

(*MRS. BEA is holding her stomach.*)

**MRS. BEA:** Oooh . . . Oooh . . . Oooh. Mrs. Munk, are you home?

**MRS. MUNK:** Why, yes, Mrs. Bea. Goodness, you seem sick. What's the trouble?

**MRS. BEA:** Sick would hardly describe my condition! I've been running from the creek, where I threw up — over to the outhouse, where . . . where . . . well, never mind.

| | |
|---|---|
| MRS. MUNK: | I get the picture! Your digestive system is all out of whack! |
| MRS. BEA: | And then some. Oooh! Oooh! |
| MRS. MUNK: | Do you know what could have caused it? |
| MRS. BEA: | Well, it was either those six sweet po -tay -toes I ate at the Mardi Gras party, or it could be that God doesn't love me anymore. Which do you think? |
| MRS. MUNK: | Let's see if I understand this. You pigged out at the party, got yourself good and sick on sweet potatoes, and now you'd like to have God be responsible for what you did. Am I getting this right? |
| MRS. BEA: | You didn't have to turn it all around like that. I was just an innocent consumer at the party. |
| MRS. MUNK: | But I saw you go back to the table for several servings and, as you say, "and then some." |
| MRS. BEA: | I guess I'm not going to get much sympathy here. I thought at least a kind word . . . |
| MRS. MUNK: | I tell you what. Instead of kind words, I'll give you a seltzer! And when your tummy feels better, you come back, and we'll talk about how much God loves you. Okay? |

(*MRS. BEA grasps her stomach again.*)

MRS. BEA:       Oooh! There it goes again. I've got to go. Bye, kids.

(*MRS. BEA hurries off stage.*)

MRS. MUNK:      I've never seen Mrs. Bea move so fast. But she really is sick. So, kids, let's have a prayer for everyone who is sick today, especially those who think God doesn't love them.

**Have Mrs. Munk pray this prayer with the children:**
Dear God, thanks for loving us. Thanks for giving us the freedom to choose how we live, even when we choose badly. And God, be with all who are sick today. Amen.

# MRS. BEA WANTS TO KNOW MORE ABOUT GOD'S LOVE

### Characters:
Mrs. Munk
Mrs. Bea

LEADER: A couple of weeks ago Mrs. Bea ate too many sweet potatoes and got pretty sick. When she asked Mrs. Munk to help, she mentioned that maybe God didn't love her anymore and this was the reason she had gotten sick. Mrs. Munk thought about this for awhile and decided she should go see Mrs. Bea.

MRS. MUNK: Oh, Mrs. Bea! Are you home, Mrs. Bea?

(*MRS. BEA comes up the steps to the stage.*)

MRS. BEA: Yes. I'm here, Mrs. Munk. And I'm glad to report that my stomach is behaving now.

MRS. MUNK: I'm glad to hear that. And that's part of the reason I came by.

MRS. BEA: You want to check out my stomach?

MRS. MUNK: Oh no, I just wanted talk with you about God's love.

| | |
|---|---|
| MRS. BEA: | God's love? |
| MRS. MUNK: | Yep, God's love. When you had that terrible stomach ache, you thought that maybe God didn't love you anymore, if my memory is correct. |
| MRS. BEA: | Oh yes. Now I remember. But I'm okay now. |
| MRS. MUNK: | I'm glad you are okay. But what about God's love? |
| MRS. BEA: | Well, I'm okay, so I don't think it's very important just now. |
| MRS. MUNK: | Now just a ding-dong minute! |
| MRS. BEA: | Whaaat? |
| MRS. MUNK: | God's love is important when things are going badly, but that same love doesn't matter when things are okay? Is that what you are saying? |
| MRS. BEA: | Ummm . . . I guess you could say that. |
| MRS. MUNK: | I'd never say that! You said that! (*Pause*) God's love is important to me all the time. My God is a twenty-four/seven God — there on days when things are going great, and standing right beside me when things go sour. I'll be seeing God's love in the spring flowers in a few days. I'll be talking to God about the beauty of spring and the meaning of Easter. |
| MRS. BEA: | Well, I talked to God too. I told God all about my upset stomach. God didn't really seem to care all that much. |

| | |
|---|---|
| MRS. MUNK: | Let's see. You talked to God about your stomach. I am one of God's servants. So God whispered to me that I should look in on you, and I happened to have medicine for your stomach. Does that seem pretty strange? |
| MRS. BEA: | Well, it might just be . . . what's the word . . . co . . . co-in . . . coincidence? (*Pause*) Do you really think God might love me enough to send someone to see about me? |
| MRS. MUNK: | I think God loves all God's children that much. I think God would like for us to take care of one another all the time, but some of us ignore the whisper. |
| MRS. BEA: | So we share God's love when we do what God wants us to do? Cool! I wonder if God has whispered to me? Kids, will you help me ask God about that? |

**Have Mrs. Bea pray this prayer with the children:**
Dear God, if you have whispered, please do that again. Let us hear your voice, and we will try to do what you ask. Bless us as we learn to listen. Amen.

# MRS. BEA TRIES TO FIND HEAVEN

### Characters:
Grumpy
Mrs. Bea

**LEADER:** After her last talk with Mrs. Munk, Mrs. Bea began to understand God's love. She was satisfied with what she was learning, until she heard some of the church members talking about "going up to heaven." She decided she'd try to get a look at the pearly gates.

**GRUMPY:** Ahem. Ahem. *Harumph!* Hi, Mrs. Bea.

**MRS. BEA:** Hi, Grumpy.

**GRUMPY:** Please, Mrs. Bea, call me — *Harumph!* — Mr. Grumpy.

**MRS. BEA:** Okay Grum — er, Mr. Grumpy.

**GRUMPY:** By the way, what brings you way up to my house on the hilltop?

**MRS. BEA:** I'm planning to climb the tallest tree on this hill. Could you show me where it is . . . er, Mr. Grumpy?

| | |
|---|---|
| GRUMPY: | Well, there's the big oak — *Harumph!* — just up ahead, and I think there's a poplar, which is even taller. It's off to the right. |
| MRS. BEA: | Yes, I see it. Well, I'll be going now. Bye, Mr. Grumpy. |
| GRUMPY: | You are going to climb that tree? It's huge! |
| MRS. BEA: | I suppose it is. And I don't guess my hands are made for something like that, but I just have to give it a try. I've got to know! |
| GRUMPY: | *Harumph!* Know what? |
| MRS. BEA: | I have to know if I can see heaven from the top of that tree. |
| GRUMPY: | You're not serious. *Harumph!* Are you? |
| MRS. BEA: | I sure am! I heard Mr. Ratchet talking to somebody at church, and he said that someday he hopes he goes up to heaven. I thought I'd go up this afternoon and just take a peek. |
| GRUMPY: | So you climbed the tallest hill around, and now you want to — *Harumph!* — go up the tallest tree on that hill . . . to get a glimpse of heaven, right? |
| MRS. BEA: | Exactly. |
| GRUMPY: | Have I — *Harumph!* — got news for you, Mrs. Bea. |
| MRS. BEA: | What do you mean? What news? |

**GRUMPY:** We've been sending men and women into space for thirty or forty years now. *Harumph!* Some to space stations, and some to the moon. They went up thousands of miles.

**MRS. BEA:** So?

**GRUMPY:** Not a one of them reported seeing any pearly gates. Grandpa told me that we use "up" to describe heaven, but we don't know exactly where heaven is . . . and only God can take us there. We sure can't see it from the top of a tree or the porthole of a spaceship. We just accept heaven on faith, like lots of other things.

**MRS. BEA:** Well, to tell the truth, I wasn't looking forward to climbing that tree. Accept it on faith, huh? There's that *faith* word again! Boys and girls, would you help me pray for enough faith to see heaven someday?

**Have Mrs. Bea pray this prayer with the children:**
Dear God, please help me to have enough faith to believe in heaven — even if I can't see it — and to get there someday. Amen.

# MRS. MUNK HEARS A VOICE

### Characters:
Mrs. Monk
Grandpa

**LEADER:** It was a nice week in Harmony. The only interesting thing until Thursday night was that a couple of the residents were talking about changing the name of the town. But it was only talk. Then came Thursday night. It was amazing — but we'll let Mrs. Munk tell that story.

**MRS. MUNK:** Grandpa . . . Wake up, Grandpa! It's Mrs. Munk.

(*GRANDPA wakes up, yawning and stretching.*)

**GRANDPA:** My gracious, Mrs. Munk! Why, it's two a.m.

**MRS. MUNK:** I know that, Grandpa. I just wanted to know why you called me?

(*GRANDPA yawns again.*)

**GRANDPA:** Excuse me . . . called you . . . Whaaat?

**MRS. MUNK:** Sure. It must have been you. It was a really old voice. And you said, "Mrs. Munk . . . Mrs. Munk . . ." I'm sure it came from this direction.

**43**

GRANDPA: Wh — When did this happen, Mrs. Munk?

MRS. MUNK: Just now . . . well, about five minutes ago.

GRANDPA: I guess you could tell it wasn't me, then. You had to wake me up to tell me about it.

MRS. MUNK: Yeah, that's right, I did. But tell me, do you talk in your sleep?

GRANDPA: I don't think so. Must have been someone else. Or maybe a dream?

MRS. MUNK: I'm sure it wasn't a dream! I came awake real fast, and I've been awake ever since. It was kind of spooky, if you know what I mean. I had the doors locked and all the little Munks tucked into bed. We had said our prayers and blown out the candles. Then at about two o'clock . . . this strange voice.

GRANDPA: Maybe it was something you ate.

MRS. MUNK: Nope. Haven't eaten anything unusual. It was a real voice, and it was calling my name.

GRANDPA: Then maybe I'm not the one you should be talking to!

MRS. MUNK: You mean it might be . . . God?

GRANDPA: Yep. Might be.

MRS. MUNK: Nah. God wouldn't talk to me. God might talk to Rev. Puggins, but not to me.

GRANDPA: Why not you?

MRS. MUNK: Well gosh, I don't know! Oh, wow. Oh, gosh. What do I do now? Now I'm really confused!

GRANDPA: You might try talking to God and then listening — and listening some more.

MRS. MUNK: Okay! Kids, will you help me with this?


**Have Mrs. Munk pray this prayer with the children:**
Dear God, if you are calling us, then we want to hear. We will listen to your words. Speak to us, Lord. Amen.

# MRS. MUNK ASKS GRUMPY ABOUT A VOICE

### Characters:
Mrs. Munk
Grumpy

**LEADER:** Mrs. Munk wasn't quite satisfied with the answers she got from Grandpa about a voice calling her name. She thought about it; prayed about it; and then talked to her good friend, Grumpy, about the voice she heard.

**MRS. MUNK:** Hi, Grumpy, how's my good friend today?

**GRUMPY:** Why, I'm just fine, Mrs. Munk. And — *Harumph!* — how are you?

**MRS. MUNK:** I'm feeling well, Grumpy, but I've got a little problem.

**GRUMPY:** I know . . . too many Munksters and too little space. Ready for me to add that room for you, Mrs. Munk? Wouldn't take long.

| | |
|---|---|
| MRS. MUNK: | Nope, it's not the kids. I don't always understand them, but this is really tough to understand. See, Grumpy, about a week ago I heard this strange voice calling my name. I thought it was Grandpa, but it wasn't him. He kind of thought it might have been . . . (*Gulp*) God. |
| GRUMPY: | God . . . gosh, that's heavy. I think God has spoken to me in lots of ways, but to have God call your name . . . wow, that is something! |
| MRS. MUNK: | But, Grumpy, I don't know what to do now. I'd like to do what God wants me to do. Do you have any advice? You are my best friend in the whole world . . . what do you think, Grumpy? |
| GRUMPY: | Um . . . oh, gosh. What did Grandpa say? |
| MRS. MUNK: | Well, he sort of said I should pray . . . and wait. What do you think? |
| GRUMPY: | I'm not real good at this, Mrs. Munk. But I'd guess that you might need to see if there is anything that might keep you from hearing what — *Harumph!* — God is saying. |
| MRS. MUNK: | You mean like dumping out all the excess stuff in my life — those things I think I have to have, so I can understand what it is that God wants for me. Is that what you are saying? |

GRUMPY:    Well — *Harumph!* — sure. You put it in better words than mine, though. But that sounds like what I was saying. You are such a nice person, God wouldn't have any trouble talking to you.

MRS. MUNK:    Somehow I don't think nice has anything to do with it, Grumpy. I think God can talk to all sorts of people, if only they will listen. But I sure do hope God will talk again . . . if that was God.

GRUMPY:    Why don't you tell God you are ready to listen? Prayer never hurts!

MRS. MUNK:    You sound like Grandpa now! Okay, I'll try again. Boys and girls, are you with me? I need your help with this.

**Have Mrs. Munk pray this prayer with the children:**
Dear God, it's me, Mrs. Munk, again, and if that was you saying my name, then speak to me again, Lord. Tell me what you want me to do. Amen.

# TEE COMPLAINS ABOUT GRANDPA'S RULES

### Characters:
Tee
Grumpy

**LEADER:** Things have quieted down in Harmony since Mrs. Munk has not heard the voice calling her name lately; and although she still wonders what it was, she has stopped talking about it. It has been quiet until Tee showed up at Grumpy's place fussing and stewing and pouting. Grumpy could tell right off that Tee was not in a good mood.

**TEE:** (*Excited; aloud to himself*) Dad gum! Blast it anyway! What does he know? Who gave him the right? He thinks he knows everything!

**GRUMPY:** Ahem — *Harumph!* — Good morning, Tee.
I wasn't really listening, but I heard you anyway. Sounds like my buddy, Tee, might be upset about something.

**TEE:** You are dillydapped right I am upset. Heck, I'm more than upset. I'm mad!

(*TEE takes a halfhearted swing at GRUMPY.*)

| GRUMPY: | Hey! Don't snap at me. I didn't do anything. I just asked what was wrong! Did I say something that made you mad? |
|---|---|
| TEE: | (*Calmer*) Sorry, Grumpy, I guess I shouldn't fuss at you, but it's that Grandpa! That old codger is really getting under my skin. |
| GRUMPY: | That sweet old — *Harumph!* — geezer? What in the world did he do? |
| TEE: | Well, you know when I came, I moved in with Grandpa . . . and that was fine. It was even fine when he told me that I'd have to have certain rules . . . I just didn't know his rules were going to be so . . . mean! |
| GRUMPY: | Gosh. Grandpa making up mean rules. *Harumph!* I don't blame you! |
| TEE: | Yeah! He told me I couldn't drive his ol' car. Heck, I just wanted to drive it up and down the driveway! It's not like I was going somewhere in it. Everybody else drives cars. Don't see why I can't! Mean old man. Makes me want to run away from home! I'm so mad I could spit . . . and maybe I will! *Ptooey!* |

(*Flick water over the curtain.*)

| GRUMPY: | Now hold on just a minute — *Harumph!* — and if you spit, aim toward the boys and girls. I've already had my shower! First thing is, I like old Grandpa. I have a lot of respect for the old geezer. He might have tough rules, but I bet he made them for your own good. |
|---|---|

| TEE: | Just because I hit that stump! He jerked me out of that old wreck of a car and told me I couldn't get behind the wheel 'till I was at least sixteen. He said maybe I could see over the steering wheel by then. |
|---|---|
| GRUMPY: | You — *Harumph!* — couldn't even see out of the windows? |
| TEE: | I didn't need to. I knew what was out there! |
| GRUMPY: | But what if one of the little munksters ran out in front of you? And what about that stump? Did you forget it? I think I understand what Grandpa is doing, and it doesn't — *Harumph!* — sound so mean to me! I think he is right in giving you rules to live by. |
| TEE: | I didn't think you'd be much help! Thanks for nothing! I thought you were my friend! |

(*TEE rushes from the stage.*)

| GRUMPY: | Wow! I'm not sure I said the right thing. Now Tee is mad at both of us. Kids, would you help me with a prayer? |

**Have Grumpy pray this prayer with the children:**
Dear God, we know we should live by rules. We know that we don't like the rules sometimes, but thank you for giving us rules to live by. And thank you for parents and guardians who care enough to give us rules. Amen.

# TEE GOES TO REV. PUGGINS

### Characters:
Tee
Rev. Puggins

**LEADER:** The little Munksters had a case of the sniffles this week, but all of them seem better now. Mrs. Munk has begun spring cleaning . . . and is thinking of making kites. But Tee — good old Tee — is still upset about the rules Grandpa gave him a few weeks ago. You remember: Tee tried to drive Grandpa's car and drove it right into a stump.

(*REV. PUGGINS is facing away from TEE.*)

**TEE:** Uh, hello, Rev. Puggins. Could I talk to you for a — could I talk to you for a minute?

**REV. PUGGINS:** (*Turning*) Oh! My goodness, it's Tee. Hi, Tee, fine day for kites, isn't it? I flew kites when I was a small . . . Why, one of them went almost out of sight . . . it was so —

**TEE:** (*Interrupting*) Rev. Puggins, I can't think about kites just now. I've got something on my mind . . . and it just won't go away!

**REV. PUGGINS:** Why, whatever could be bothering a fine fellow like you?

| | |
|---|---|
| TEE: | Well, it's this thing with Grandpa. I guess you heard about it. The church grapevine seems to know everything. I guess the voice mail is working! |
| REV. PUGGINS: | Ummm . . . oh, you must mean the little incident with Grandpa's car and the tree stump, and his new rule? Is that what's bothering you? |
| TEE: | Exactly! And I hate to admit it, but I haven't even spoken to him since that day he laid down his rules. He talks to me, but I just stare at him! |
| REV. PUGGINS: | So you have come to me . . . for what? |
| TEE: | Well, I went to see Grumpy, and I went to see Mrs. Munk, but they just took up for Grandpa! I thought you'd at least be fair about it. |
| REV. PUGGINS: | Now, let's see, your problem seems to be . . . seems to be with Grandpa. Seems as though you folks need to talk. And when you are just pouting or sullen or withdrawn, that problem isn't going away. Why, I remember a similar case — |
| TEE: | You do? How'd it come out? Did the boy win? Did the father lose? |
| REV. PUGGINS: | It's really kind of hard to say who won. The boy was named Jacob, and he broke some rules . . . tricked his dad . . . and then had to leave town. But you know what he discovered a while later? |
| TEE: | No, what? |

REV. PUGGINS:  He found out that the answers to his questions — or maybe we could say his destiny were back at home. And his life wouldn't get straightened out until he headed back toward home.

TEE:  So what are you saying, Rev. Puggins? I heard about Jacob in Sunday school — but what does it have to do with me?

REV. PUGGINS:  It has everything to do with you, Tee. The answers you are looking for aren't here. They are back at home with Grandpa. I think you need to go see him, Tee. And this time, open up that great big mouth and talk!

REV. PUGGINS:  Now, let's have a prayer. Boys and girls. would you join us?

**Have Rev. Puggins pray this prayer with the children:**
Dear God, help us move beyond the anger that keeps us apart. And help Tee find his way home. Amen.

# PALM SUNDAY IN HARMONY

### Characters:
Tee

Mrs. Munk

| | |
|---|---|
| **LEADER:** | Oh, it was wonderful, Palm Sunday was. The church was decorated with wildflowers, the clearing had been swept clean. Rev. Puggins delivered an inspiring message, and the little Harmony church celebrated! In the midst of their celebrating, Tee caught Mrs. Munk at the edge of the clearing . . . |
| **TEE:** | Hey, Mrs. Munk, just a second. |
| **MRS. MUNK:** | Well, hi, Tee. I'm so glad to hear that you and Grandpa are friends again! |
| **TEE:** | Oh, yeah. But that's not why I stopped you. |
| **MRS. MUNK:** | Oh . . . then what's on your mind, Tee? |
| **TEE:** | Well, it's this . . . We just had this big hoopla at church . . . folks waving branches, lots of flowers, youth and adult choirs singing. And Rev. Puggins must have preached for forty-five minutes! What the dickens was going on? |

| | |
|---|---|
| MRS. MUNK: | Do you remember how our church bulletin said, "Palm Sunday?" |
| TEE: | Yep, I noticed that. So what? |
| MRS. MUNK: | Palm Sunday helps us remember when Jesus rode into Jerusalem, Tee. For a few minutes it looked like everybody really liked him! They shouted "Hosanna! Hosanna!" And they waved tree branches like we did in our service. It was a nice moment and must have been like a celebration. Can you say "Hosanna!", Tee? |
| TEE: | (*In a very small voice*) Hosanna. |
| MRS. MUNK: | That wasn't very impressive, Tee. Can't you do any better to welcome Jesus? |
| TEE: | Hosanna. |
| MRS. MUNK: | That still doesn't sound like you are saying hi to the king! How would you welcome, say . . . Michael Jordan or the president? |
| TEE: | Oh, gosh, I'd try to out-shout everybody else, like, "Hellooo! Welcome to Harmony!" And boy, I'd be loud! |
| MRS. MUNK: | So you can get pretty loud! Now, imagine Jesus. He is coming down the path toward Harmony. Could you greet him with a nice "Hosanna!"? |

**TEE:** Uh, yeah. I think so! Hosanna . . . nope, not enough . . . Hosanna! Still not quite enough, because he is so special. Hosssaaannna! Welcome, Jesus!

**MRS. MUNK:** That's the spirit! Now, could you lead the boys and girls as they learn to welcome Jesus?

**TEE:** Sure, they learn fast! Okay, boys and girls, on three. One, two, three: Hosanna. Not good enough. One, two, three: Hosanna! Still not good enough. Help me with this. One, two, three: Hosssaaannna! Now shout, "Welcome, Lord Jesus!" Amen.

# TEE'S CONFUSION ABOUT THE EMPTY TOMB

## Characters:
Tee
Grandpa

**LEADER:** Tee has been thinking about Easter and the empty tomb. Grandpa had tried to tell him the events in a very simple form. I don't think Tee has the right idea yet.

**TEE:** Hey, Grandpa, is breakfast ready yet?

**GRANDPA:** Not quite, Tee. But come on in. It's almost done.

**TEE:** It was a nice morning for an Easter egg hunt, Grandpa. That rabbit hid a lot of eggs in our yard, didn't he?

**GRANDPA:** (*Chuckling*) Yep, I guess he did. And Easter is always a nice morning, Tee. Even if the weather is bad, it's a fine morning.

**TEE:** Why do you say that, Grandpa?

**GRANDPA:** Don't you remember the little story I told you, that story about water bugs and dragonflies?

TEE: Oh yeah, the one about water bugs scurrying around until it's time for them to . . . to . . .

GRANDPA: To go to the surface and make cocoons, so they can become dragonflies.

TEE: So Easter is the time we celebrate Jesus going into a cocoon?

GRANDPA: No, Tee, Jesus was buried in a tomb on a Friday afternoon; and on Sunday morning he came out of that tomb, alive! That's what Easter is about.

TEE: So he didn't become a dragonfly?

GRANDPA: No. I think he must have become some sort of a spirit person. His poor body had been tortured on that cross. But on Sunday morning the tomb was empty. Jesus was alive. He went around visiting his friends, telling them not to be worried. You see, he had already told them that he was going to fix up a place for each one in heaven.

TEE: Yeah, I remember now. And you know what, Grandpa?

GRANDPA: What, Tee?

TEE: The next time I'm down at the pond, I'm going to ask the dragonflies to fix us a real nice room in heaven.

GRANDPA: I'm afraid you still don't quite have it right, Tee. But I guess it won't hurt for you to tell the dragonflies to fix you a room.

TEE: Oh, yeah. And when I'm down there, I'll explain to them how the Easter bunny dug out this nice tomb for Jesus and then left a trail of candy and eggs so he could find it. I bet the dragonflies would like to know the whole story.

GRANDPA: It's going to take a while to get this untangled, Tee. Breakfast is ready, so wash up. But before you do, let's offer our thanks. Kids, would you help?

**Have Grandpa pray this prayer with the children:**
Dear God, it's Easter morning. We want to thank you for Jesus — for the life he led, for that empty tomb, and for his promise that we'd live forever. Amen.

# MRS. MUNK AND THE RESURRECTION

## Character:
Mrs. Munk

**LEADER:** Just last week we celebrated Easter in Harmony. Mrs. Munk showed up at the Bible study with a frown on her face. She'd been a church member for years, but when she caught up with me on the way home, she had some important questions.

**MRS. MUNK:** Could you wait just a moment! You've got those long legs, and I'm afraid I'm vertically challenged.

**LEADER:** Sure, Mrs. Munk. I'd be glad to walk along with you.

**MRS. MUNK:** And watch where you put those big feet. If you stepped on me . . . I hate to think. It could be curtains . . . I could kick the bucket . . . shuffle off this mortal coil . . . cross the river —

**LEADER:** (*Interrupting*) I get the picture.

**MRS. MUNK:** Well, your feet should be registered as deadly weapons. What size are they, anyway? Looks like maybe fourteens.

| | |
|---|---|
| LEADER: | These are just tens, Mrs. Munk. I'll watch where I walk, okay? |
| MRS. MUNK: | Okay. But the idea of you squashing me brings me to a question. It's something I've been wondering about. You seem to have some knowledge of this stuff, so I wanted to ask you. |
| LEADER: | What, Mrs. Munk? |
| MRS. MUNK: | When Jesus rose from the dead, did he come back as a spirit or as a real person? |
| LEADER: | Now that's a tough question. I think that he might have had both forms. Soon after the Resurrection he told one of his friends not to touch him because he had not yet risen to the Father. Later on he was seen cooking fish beside a lake. Then when he met Thomas, he told him to touch the places where he had been wounded. At times he seemed to have been spirit; other times he seemed very real. Does that help? |
| MRS. MUNK: | So he came back as both? |
| LEADER: | That's the way it seems. And when we call our church "the Body of Christ," then he has life in still another way. |
| MRS. MUNK: | Whew, this is getting complicated. And I was going to explain it to the Munksters. |

LEADER:     And we aren't quite through. When you are at your very best and your most loving, then other people can see Jesus in what you do or say. That's another way he lives. It's not an easy thing to understand, is it?

MRS. MUNK:  It sure isn't! I hadn't even thought about people seeing Jesus in the things I say or do. That makes me wonder something else.

LEADER:     What's that?

MRS. MUNK:  I wonder if I shouldn't ask for help? And if the kids will join in, I'll do just that.

**Have Mrs. Munk pray this prayer with the children:**
Dear God, help me to be like Jesus so all my friends will know that Jesus is still alive in my heart. Amen.

# INQUIRING MINDS

### Characters:
Tee
Grandpa

**LEADER:** Easter had arrived just last week. It was a wonderful day. The little brush arbor was packed. After the service Tee caught up with Grandpa and had some questions for him.

(*GRANDPA is walking across the stage. TEE appears behind him.*)

**TEE:** Wait up, Grandpa!

(*GRANDPA is startled; he turns around abruptly.*)

**GRANDPA:** Oh, hi, Tee. I was just thinking about our Easter service. Wasn't it just glorious?

**TEE:** Yeah, I guess so. That's why I stopped you.

**GRANDPA:** Oh?

**TEE:** I have been wondering about this empty tomb thing. Why did everybody get so excited over something that's empty? I mean, what's that all about?

| | |
|---|---|
| GRANDPA: | Well, Tee, the empty tomb doesn't excite because it's empty. It excites us because Jesus is not in that tomb. |
| TEE: | Oh, he went somewhere else? |
| GRANDPA: | He sure did. That tomb couldn't hold him. He returned to life. We call it the Resurrection. And then he started showing up to different people. |
| TEE: | I'd be scared. I would think he was a ghost. |
| GRANDPA: | I expect lots of folks were scared. But he'd tell them it was okay, and they didn't need to worry. Then he'd ask questions or send them out to do his work. |
| TEE: | So the tomb just says, "He's not in here anymore. He's not dead anymore. He's out with his people!" |
| GRANDPA: | Exactly, Tee. I think you are catching on. This is a really, really important part of our faith. |
| TEE: | I thought it must be, with all the pretty flowers and nice music and stuff. |
| GRANDPA: | Well, I want you to think about what all this means, Tee. He died for us and came back to life. He's still around, and he wants us to have a life that goes on forever . . . just like his. I think you are getting close to understanding faith, Tee. |

| TEE: | I'm trying to understand, Grandpa. It's not always easy, though. |
|---|---|
| GRANDPA: | Real faith has never been easy, Tee. Let's say a prayer with these kids and ask God to help us as we grow in faith. |

**Have Grandpa pray this prayer with the children:**
Dear God, sometimes faith is hard — hard to understand and hard to keep — so we ask you to help us through those hard places. Amen.

# REV. PUGGINS AND GRUMPY TALK ABOUT GRANDPA

### Characters:
Rev. Puggins
Grumpy

**LEADER:** Last week Tee found out that Grandpa was moving to Orlando. Tee was pretty upset until Grandpa offered to take him along. They are busy packing now, but some of the Harmony folks are still talking about Grandpa.

**REV. PUGGINS:** I guess you heard the news, Grumpy.

**GRUMPY:** *Harumph!* I sure did, Rev. Puggins. Can't say that I like it, though.

**REV. PUGGINS:** None of us like it, Grumpy, but it's sort of like . . . uh . . . life.

**GRUMPY:** Now, what does that mean?

**REV. PUGGINS:** Grumpy, the preacher in the Book of Ecclesiastes says there is a season and a time for everything. I suppose this is the season for Grandpa to move and the time for us to miss him.

| GRUMPY: | That doesn't make it easier. |
|---|---|
| REV. PUGGINS: | It's never easy to give up folks who have become part of your family. And we'll always remember Grandpa and Tee. |
| GRUMPY: | Grandpa said something like that a long time ago. He was talking about how his body was aging. I remember that. |
| REV. PUGGINS: | Do you remember how Grandpa helped Mrs. Bea when she arrived? |
| GRUMPY: | Sure. And I remember how — *Harumph!* — Grandpa showed me how to treat other folks in a nice way. I used to be a bully. He helped me understand. |
| REV. PUGGINS: | And do you remember what Grandpa said about Christmas? |
| GRUMPY: | Oh, yeah! And he showed me my first Christmas tree. Then that Tee showed up, and he was so scared of me! Isn't that funny? *Harumph!* Tee was scared of me! |
| REV. PUGGINS: | That didn't last very long, did it? |
| GRUMPY: | No! He was here for just a week or two, and then he was hugging me . . . it was almost embarrassing! |

REV. PUGGINS:     Tee is a fine boy. Do you remember how concerned he was when Hurricane Floyd hit some of his friends in North Carolina? He helped us contribute to those people in a time of real need.

GRUMPY:     *Harumph!* I remember. I remember so much! Those two gave us a lot to remember.

REV. PUGGINS:     Let's thank God for Grandpa and Tee and everyone who gives us wonderful memories.

**Have Rev. Puggins pray this prayer with the children:**
Dear God, thanks for all the folks who give us fine memories. Stay close to them, wherever they are. Amen.

# MRS. BEA MEETS MR. RATCHET

### Characters:
Mr. Ratchet
Mrs. Bea

LEADER: Grandpa and Tee are almost done packing for their move to Orlando. There is a lot of noise coming from their house as they shuffle furniture and move boxes around. But today there is a new noise in Harmony . . . and several people stuck their heads out to see what it was. Mrs. Bea was most curious.

(*MR. RATCHET is loudly whistling the tune to "Morning Has Broken."*)

MRS. BEA: What in the world? That's a new noise! I guess it's not a bad noise. But it's new around here.

(*MR. RATCHET stops whistling and looks around.*)

MR. RATCHET: Oh, hello. Was I disturbing you?

MRS. BEA: Well, maybe you were, and maybe you weren't. Did you intend to disturb me?

MR. RATCHET: Gosh, no. I just whistle when I'm happy, and this is one of those times.

| MRS. BEA: | I see. You won't let it happen again, will you? |
|---|---|
| MR. RATCHET: | Ummm, you mean I won't be happy again, or I won't whistle again? |
| MRS. BEA: | That . . . that disturbing the peace thing you were doing. You call that infernal noise whistling? |
| MR. RATCHET: | It's whistling, all right. Haven't you ever heard a nice whistler? |

(*MR. RATCHET begins whistling again, louder this time.*)

| MRS. BEA: | Okay, okay . . . enough! So, you are some kind of bird? |
|---|---|
| MR. RATCHET: | You won't see any feathers on me! I'm not a bird. I just like to whistle. I suppose that's why they gave me my nickname. |
| MRS. BEA: | And what is your nickname? |
| MR. RATCHET: | Folks where I come from call me Mr. Racket. Yep, that's me . . . Mr. Racket. My real name is Ratchet. I'm a newcomer, and I'm thinking about moving to this area; in fact, I found a nice home just over there. |

(*MR. RATCHET motions in the distance.*)

| MRS. BEA: | But . . . but that's right over next to my house. |
|---|---|
| MR. RATCHET: | Oh? Then I must be your new neighbor! |

MRS. BEA:    B . . . b . . . But I like to sleep late, and I nap in the afternoon. And . . . and I'm just not sure this will work out . . . not sure at all!

MR. RATCHET:    See you later, neighbor. I'm going to check out my new home.

(*MR. RATCHET exits.*)

MRS. BEA:    Oh, boys and girls, What am I going to do? I have such a nice home, and now this noisy creature is moving in right beside me. Do you think prayer might help?

**Have Mrs. Bea pray this prayer with the children:**
Dear God, I'm pretty upset. I had such a nice life; now everything is ruined. Help me deal with this. And if you really want me to, make me into a good neighbor. Amen.

# DEEP BLUE MOODS IN HARMONY

### Characters:
Mrs. Munk
Grumpy

### Prop:
small bits of straw

LEADER: There hasn't been any word yet from Tee and Grandpa. They moved on to Orlando and a new kind of life. They left behind lots of friends and some fine memories. It was not long after they moved that Mrs. Munk noticed that a certain person was not being seen around Harmony

MRS. MUNK: (*Huffing and puffing*) Grumpy! I say, Grumpy! Are you up on this hilltop somewhere, Grumpy?

GRUMPY: (*Muted voice*) Oh, hi, Mrs. Munk.

(*GRUMPY is still out of sight.*)

MRS. MUNK: Grumpy, you get out here right now!

(*After a long pause, GRUMPY emerges with straw stuck to his clothing.*)

GRUMPY:     Hi, Mrs. Munk. What's up?

MRS. MUNK:  Well! You certainly aren't up! Sleeping in again,
            Grumpy? And just look at you!

GRUMPY:     Yeah, I — *Harumph!* — guess so.

MRS. MUNK:  Isn't that something new, Grumpy . . . sleeping in,
            I mean?

GRUMPY:     Yeah, I — *Harumph!* — guess so.

MRS. MUNK:  What have you done with the real Grumpy? You
            don't look or sound like my good friend! Now
            where is he?

GRUMPY:     *Harumph!* I don't know what you mean, Mrs.
            Munk.

MRS. MUNK:  I mean that you look a mess, you are sleeping
            a lot now, and the best thing you can say is,
            "Yeah, I guess so." My friend Grumpy doesn't
            act or talk that way. Now what have you done
            with him?

(*GRUMPY snickers and almost laughs.*)

GRUMPY:     That's — *Harumph!* — funny, Mrs. Munk. You
            know I'm Grumpy. Always have been . . . always
            will be!

**74**

MRS. MUNK: No, I think my friend Grumpy has been replaced by this old sad sack who misses Grandpa and Tee, but won't talk about it. I think my friend Grumpy is hiding in there somewhere, and this old sad lookalike has taken over. I want my friend! What have you done with Grumpy?

(*GRUMPY giggles.*)

GRUMPY: I — *Harumph!* — guess you are right, Mrs. Munk: I came up here to my cabin right after Grandpa and Tee left. I — *Harumph!* — guess I just forgot to eat or comb my hair or get out of bed. I just feel rotten, Mrs. Munk. I miss those two so much.

(*MRS. MUNK hugs GRUMPY.*)

MRS. MUNK: We all miss them, Grumpy. I missed them an awful lot . . . and then I started missing you! And there was no reason to miss you! Made me wonder if something was wrong with you. Now I see that you have a case of the blues.

GRUMPY: The blues? Is it catching? Do I need an aspirin? Am I running a fever?

MRS. MUNK: Grumpy, the blues . . . well, it's what happens when we lose someone or something that has been very important to us. And it's okay to grieve those losses. They are real, and they do hurt!

GRUMPY:      But when will I stop missing them, Mrs. Munk?

MRS. MUNK:   We never do stop missing those we lose, Grumpy.
             They have been a part of our lives; and though we
             miss them, life moves on, and we visit them in
             our memories.

GRUMPY:      Would it be okay if I said a prayer for Grandpa
             and Tee and all those folks we miss so much?

MRS. MUNK:   That would be wonderful, Grumpy.


**Have Grumpy pray this prayer with the children:**
Dear God, sometimes we forget to tell people we love them until
it is too late. Help us to remember. Be with all our friends and
family who are far away from us today. Amen.

# GRUMPY: IS A LITTLE WHITE LIE SUCH A BAD THING?

## Characters:
Grumpy
Mrs. Munk

**LEADER:** Rev. Puggins had preached a powerful sermon down in the clearing outside Harmony. He had finished up with the idea that Christianity was a full-time job, and we didn't need any part-time Christians. Grumpy had listened closely to what was being said, and it bothered him. He caught up with Mrs. Munk on the way home from church.

(*MRS. MUNK is bumping along, humming "Amazing Grace" to herself, as though going home. GRUMPY appears at far right.*)

**GRUMPY:** Hey, Mrs. Munk. *Harumph!* Wait a minute, will you?

**MRS. MUNK:** Sure, Grumpy, I'll always wait for my favorite fellow! What's up?

**GRUMPY:** Well, Mrs. Munk, I heard — *Harumph!* — old Rev. Puggins saying that we should be full-time Christians. In fact, I think I heard him say that about — *Harumph!* — four times!

| MRS. MUNK: | I imagine you did, Grumpy. That was a very important idea. And Rev. Puggins really emphasizes the important things. Did it bother you or something? |
|---|---|
| GRUMPY: | Well, I — *Harumph!* — guess so. You see, once in a while I tell a little white lie. Like last week I chased the kids out of my yard. It wasn't like I was going to hurt one of them. I just enjoy chasing them. But when Mrs. Bea asked if that was me she saw chasing the kids, I . . . I . . . I lied about it! *Harumph!* Is a little white lie okay every now and then? Please tell me it's okay! *Harumph!* I feel pretty bad about it! |
| MRS. MUNK: | I can't say it's okay, Grumpy, because it's not. God tells us the truth all the time, and God wants us to tell the truth. Lies hurt. Grumpy, think about it. Would it be okay if you stuck your hand into a campfire, just once in a while? It would still hurt, wouldn't it? Lying is just about like that. Somebody is usually getting hurt. And it is usually the person who tells the lie. |
| GRUMPY: | *Harumph!* Gosh, I hadn't thought about it that way. Now I really feel bad! I guess I shouldn't have blamed my cousin. He wasn't even — *Harumph!* — near Harmony! Now I have to face him, and Mrs. Bea too! |
| MRS. MUNK: | That's right, Grumpy. Lies don't really help things at all. Why don't you ask the boys and girls to help you with this as you speak to God in prayer? |

GRUMPY:     B . . . b . . . b . . . but, Mrs. Munk, I prayed just last week. Didn't I, kids?

(*Encourage the children to nod their heads.*)

MRS. MUNK:     Grumpy, Rev. Puggins said he wanted full-time Christians! That means praying a lot more than once a week! Go on, now.

GRUMPY:     Okay, but I'll need your help, boys and girls. Will you help me?

**Have Grumpy pray this prayer with the children:**
Dear God, it is not easy to be a Christian all the time, but we want to. Help us as we grow up in your way. Amen.

# GRUMPY ASKS MRS. MUNK HOW HE CAN BE CLOSER TO GOD

## Characters:
Grumpy
Mrs. Munk

**LEADER:** After Mrs. Munk showed the boys and girls a ladder, like Jacob's ladder, Grumpy showed up at her home . . . and ol' Grumpy had questions, like he usually does.

**GRUMPY:** Mrs. Munk . . . Hey, Mrs. Munk! It's your good friend — *Harumph!* — Grumpy! I need to talk with you, Mrs. Munk.

**MRS. MUNK:** My goodness, Grumpy, you certainly seem to be in a hurry. You're not in some kind of trouble, are you? You haven't been chasing the kids again, have you?

**GRUMPY:** Why, Mrs. Munk, how could you think such a — *Harumph!* — thing?

**MRS. MUNK:** Grumpy, I could think such a thing because I know you; and I know that even though you want to do right, it isn't always easy.

**GRUMPY:** Now that you mention it — *Harumph!* — I guess that's why I'm here. You see, sometimes I don't feel very close to God. And I tried to climb up Jacob's ladder last week — *Harumph!* — but I fell off, right on my behind. So, Mrs. Munk, what do you suggest? How can I — and how can my young friends down there — get closer to God?

**MRS. MUNK:** Fell right off Jacob's ladder, huh? Well, that's not an easy one to climb. I tell you what, Grumpy. I have sensed that you have a little trouble praying. Is that right?

**GRUMPY:** Well, I bow my head like this, put my hands together . . . but the words just don't — *Harumph!* — come out. I can talk with you about God, but I sure have trouble talking with God about me.

**MRS. MUNK:** Grumpy, if you can talk to me, then you can talk to God. Tell God when you fall on your behind. Tell God when you don't understand. Tell God when you have trouble praying, and I bet the words will just flow. Will you try that, Grumpy?

**GRUMPY:** *Harumph!* Sure. I'd try almost anything!

**MRS. MUNK:** Then you can start by leading the boys and girls in prayer right now, okay?

**GRUMPY:** *Harumph!* You mean this very minute?

MRS. MUNK:    Yes.

GRUMPY:    Okay . . . Are you with me, boys and girls? Here we go.

**Have Grumpy pray this prayer with the children:**
Dear God, this is Grumpy talking. I don't always know what to say. I try to be good . . . I try to be kind. God, I love you. I guess that's all.

MRS. MUNK:    Amen.

# GRUMPY FINDS A MOM

### Characters:
Grumpy
Mrs. Munk


**LEADER:** Mother's Day arrived in Harmony with a big dinner and lots of flowers. Some of the folks wore red flowers to honor mothers who were living, and some wore white flowers to honor mothers who had died. It was a day filled with memories for everyone . . . memories of moms who had done so much. Well, almost everyone. There was one guy who seemed like he wasn't joining in.

**MRS. MUNK:** Hi, Grumpy. Isn't this a lovely Mother's Day?

**GRUMPY:** *Harumph!* I guess so.

**MRS. MUNK:** Of course it is, but my friend Grumpy seems to have an attitude today. What's wrong, Grumpy?

**GRUMPY:** Oh, nothing . . . nothing at all.

**MRS. MUNK:** Come on now, Grumpy, this is Mrs. Munk you are talking to. And I can always tell when you have an attitude. Now, what is it? Come on, tell me what's wrong.

GRUMPY: Oh, it's just that . . . *Harumph!* Nah, never mind.

MRS. MUNK: Grumpy . . .

GRUMPY: Okay. Mrs. Munk, everybody is celebrating Mother's Day today.

(*GRUMPY covers his face with his hands.*)

GRUMPY: I . . . I . . . I can't even remember my mother, Mrs. Munk. My mom died when I was — *Harumph!* — about eight weeks old. I feel really sad when everybody else has a mom, and I don't.

MRS. MUNK: Hmmm. Let me think for a moment. (*Pauses*) Stop squirming, kids, I'm trying to think. (*Pauses*) I've got an idea, Grumpy. It might be just what you need!

GRUMPY: What's that, Mrs. Munk?

MRS. MUNK: Have you ever heard of adoption, Grumpy?

GRUMPY: Yep. *Harumph!* So what?

MRS. MUNK: I know we don't look much alike. And I know some folks will think I'm crazy; but, Grumpy, if you really want a mom, I'll adopt you! I love you already. You know that, and love is part of being a good mom. Yep, I'll just adopt you, and then you'll have a mom, and my Munksters will have a new brother!

| GRUMPY: | Would you really? I mean, wow! *Harumph!* I'd have a real mom who loves me! That would be so great! |
|---|---|
| MRS. MUNK: | There are a couple of things we'll have to work out. For one, I don't think you can fit in the Munkster's bedroom, so we might have to build a bedroom. Yep, this will work out just fine! |
| GRUMPY: | I never dreamed that I'd have a real mom . . . I'm so happy I could spit. |
| MRS. MUNK: | (*Interrupting*) That's quite all right, Grumpy. I've seen you spit before. Maybe a prayer would be better. Could you do that if the boys and girls help? |
| GRUMPY: | I'd really rather sing. But, okay, if the kids will help. Here goes. |

**Have Grumpy pray this prayer with the children:**
Dear God — *Harumph!* — thank you for moms, and for all those folks who love us like moms. Amen.

# GRUMPY ASKS MRS. MUNK ABOUT REPENTING

### Characters:
Grumpy
Mrs. Munk

**LEADER:** Harmony had been pretty quiet. Mrs. Munk had gotten a postcard from Grandpa that said he was doing okay. She read it to all the other critters during the church service. The last line of the postcard said, "Ask the folks if they know how to repent, because that's very important." Then he signed it, "Love, Grandpa." A couple of hours later, Grumpy made his way to Mrs. Munk's house.

**GRUMPY:** Mrs. Munk, it's your friend, Grumpy. I'm at your front door, Mrs. Munk!

**MRS. MUNK:** (*From offstage*) Just a moment, Grumpy. I'm getting all the little Munksters to bed for their afternoon nap. I'll be right with you.

(*MRS. MUNK walks up the steps to the stage area.*)

**MRS. MUNK:** There, all through. Now, what can I do for you today, Grumpy?

GRUMPY: Well, Mrs. Munk, I heard Rev. Puggins talking about the need to repent and sin no more. *Harumph!* But then I heard some teenagers talking about how Rev. Puggins needed to put a second coat of paint on his house. The first one had too much paint thinner. One of them said he should "repaint and thin no more!" Hee hee hee . . . isn't that funny, Mrs. Munk? Repaint and thin no more!

MRS. MUNK: Yes, that's pretty funny. But repenting is serious business, Grumpy. We can say I'm sorry without changing our lives very much. In fact, we can be sorry for the things we do each and every week. But repenting and sinning no more means that we are not only sorry, but also that we are going to change our behavior so that it just doesn't happen again.

GRUMPY: You've tried to convince me that I shouldn't chase away the kids out of my yard anymore. *Harumph!* In fact, I felt sorry when one of them fell and broke a leg while I was chasing them . . . and if I repent of this act, then I'll have to really fight all my instincts. *Harumph!* I wonder if I can do this and still be a real person?

MRS. MUNK: Of course you would be a real person, Grumpy. You'd just be a much nicer person, and maybe you'd have some new friends in that child's family.

GRUMPY: Well, I'll have to really think and pray about all this. I still think "repaint and thin no more" is pretty funny! *Harumph!*

MRS. MUNK: Oh, Grumpy . . . Sometimes I think you'll never learn! I think I'll ask the boys and girls if I can lead a prayer for everyone who is sorry about something, but has real trouble repenting; and that includes you! Boys and girls, will you help him?

**Have Mrs. Munk pray this prayer with the children:**
Dear God, repentance is a hard thing. It is easy to joke about, but it is hard to do. Bless us when we truly repent. Amen.

# GRUMPY HEARS A RUMOR

### Characters:
Grumpy
Mrs. Munk

LEADER:     We don't know where the rumor started. It seems to have been passed along by the gossip line. Grumpy heard some of the rumors, which really got him excited.

GRUMPY:     (*Out of breath*) Mrs. Munk! *Harumph!* Mrs. Munk! Did you hear it, Mrs. Munk?

MRS. MUNK:     (*Yawning*) Hear what, Grumpy? Oh my goodness, it's almost midnight!

GRUMPY:     I'm sorry to wake you. But I just heard . . . the most exciting news!

MRS. MUNK:     At midnight? Oh, come on, Grumpy. Nobody hears good news at midnight.

GRUMPY:     This was — *Harumph!* — the very best kind of news, Mrs. Munk.

MRS. MUNK:     And you just heard it?

GRUMPY:     Yes, isn't it — *Harumph!* — great?

MRS. MUNK: (*Yawning again*) I hope so. But you haven't told me what the news is or how you heard it.

GRUMPY: You — *Harumph!* — ever heard of voice mail, Mrs. Munk?

MRS. MUNK: Yes, but I didn't know you had —

GRUMPY: (*Interrupting*) I don't mean that old — *Harumph!* — recorded stuff. I mean real voice mail!

MRS. MUNK: Real voice mail?

GRUMPY: My family has been sending voice mail — *Harumph!* — for years. We just pass along what we hear, by calling each other on the phone.

MRS. MUNK: I think I get the picture. So you got this voice mail?

GRUMPY: Yep, it was very faint. Bad connection, I think. I almost couldn't hear it . . . it was from one of my cousins way down near Orlando. It wasn't much of a message, but — *Harumph!* — gosh, was it exciting!

MRS. MUNK: (*Yawning again*) I suppose you are going to tell me what your voice mail said?

GRUMPY: I was almost asleep — *Harumph!* — then I heard this cousin, way off, and if I heard him right, the message was, "Tell Grumpy that Grandpa's coming."

| | |
|---|---|
| MRS. MUNK: | What? Grandpa is coming back to Harmony? |
| GRUMPY: | I think that's what the message said. I think I got it right. |
| MRS. MUNK: | You're sure it wasn't, "Tell Grumpy to go back to bed," or something like that? |
| GRUMPY: | I don't think so. I think I heard, "Tell Grumpy that Grandpa's coming." |
| MRS. MUNK: | Wouldn't that be a wonder? I've missed his old scraggly beard and that big mouth. But I've missed his good sense and his faith a lot more. I hope he does come back. |
| GRUMPY: | Me too! Me too! Makes me feel like a kid again! Would it be okay if I say a prayer for Grandpa? Kids, would you help? |

**Have Grumpy pray this prayer with the children:**
Dear God, thank you for our friends, whether they are near or far away. Thank you for adults who help us know what is real and what is not. Amen.

# GRUMPY CELEBRATES FATHER'S DAY

### Characters:
Grumpy
Mr. Ratchet

**LEADER:** Father's Day has come, and it's time to celebrate dads. Let's listen in on Mr. Ratchet and Grumpy as they talk about their fathers.

**GRUMPY:** *Harumph!* Hey, Mr. Ratchet. What's up?

**MR. RATCHET:** Nothing much, just taking some flowers to the cemetery. I'm going to put them at my father's grave.

**GRUMPY:** Be — *Harumph!* — okay if I walk along with you?

**MR. RATCHET:** Sure. How are you going to celebrate Father's Day?

**GRUMPY:** I thought I'd chase a few kids out of my yard. My dad did that too.

**MR. RATCHET:** I see.

GRUMPY: I'm pretty good at it . . . must be the best thing my dad taught me. He said, "Just get a broom or a rake and go after them." I wasn't very good at it at first. But now kids run all the way into town. It's great!

MR. RATCHET: I believe it!

GRUMPY: And something else . . . I'm — *Harumph!* — going to send a card to Grandpa. *Harumph!* He's been like a father to me. Mrs. Munk says that it is okay. He's not dead. *Harumph!* I can talk to him whenever I want to.

MR. RATCHET: So you have two fathers? Now, that is wonderful.

GRUMPY: Well, I really have three.

MR. RATCHET: Three?

GRUMPY: Yep. Grandpa taught me about my third father. He's in heaven.

MR. RATCHET: Oh . . . so is my father.

GRUMPY: But this one is the boss of heaven.

MR. RATCHET: Boss of . . . heaven?

GRUMPY: Oh, come on now, Mr. Ratchet! *Harumph!* I'm talking about God — my heavenly father, your heavenly father, and everybody's heavenly father, and the boss of heaven.

MR. RATCHET:     I hadn't thought about remembering God on
                 Father's Day. Maybe I can leave a couple of
                 flowers down at our little church. You think God
                 would like that?

GRUMPY:          I think so. And maybe we could — *Harumph!* —
                 remember him in a prayer too.


**Have Grumpy pray this prayer with the children:**
Dear God . . . Father of us all . . . We thank you for all good
men — men who teach us so much, for our fathers, and —
*Harumph!* — We really, really thank you for being our loving
father. Amen.

# STEPHEN MUST HAVE BEEN CRAZY

### Characters:
Mrs. Bea
Mrs. Munk

**LEADER:** As the season of Pentecost continues, Rev. Puggins selected Scripture that mentioned a disciple named Stephen. The sermon was about a remarkable change in the life of a man named Saul . . . but Mrs. Bea was still thinking about Stephen as she walked home from the worship service.

**MRS. BEA:** I think we just heard a story about a real nut case!

**MRS. MUNK:** Saul? Are you talking about the man who became the apostle Paul? Why, he gave us many books of the Bible and inspired us with all his missionary journeys. I don't really think that Saul —

**MRS. BEA:** (*Interrupting*) No, silly, not Saul, or Paul, or whatever you call him. The other guy, the one they threw the rocks at . . . what was his name?

**MRS. MUNK:** Oh, you mean Stephen?

**MRS. BEA:** Yep . . . a true nut case from the word go!

| | |
|---|---|
| MRS. MUNK: | Why in the world would you say that? |
| MRS. BEA: | Because he just asked for trouble! He didn't have to admit that he was a Christian, but oh no . . . he just goes and blabs it out loud for all the world to hear! A normal person would have just fibbed and run away. |
| MRS. MUNK: | Maybe Christians aren't what you consider normal. |
| MRS. BEA: | Do you mean to tell me there are other people like that? |
| MRS. MUNK: | There have been thousands throughout the ages who died rather than deny their faith. I bet you can remember the girl who said she did believe in God, just before she was killed by another student. She had what church folks call the "courage of her convictions." Her faith and courage have inspired thousands of people across this country. |
| MRS. BEA: | Seems like a pretty high price to pay, just to be a Christian! |
| MRS. MUNK: | Everybody doesn't pay that kind of price, but everybody does have moments in life when their faith is on the line, and we have to make hard decisions. Sometimes we lose friends when they try to get us to do bad things, and we decide that we need to follow Jesus instead. I guess it's a lot easier just to go along with the crowd . . . and sometimes it's very hard to be a Christian. Stephen knew all about that! |

| | |
|---|---|
| MRS. BEA: | Still sounds pretty crazy to me. |
| MRS. MUNK: | But if your beliefs are really important; and if you truly love God and his son, Jesus, then you find the courage to do what is right. And when you do what is right, you follow the footsteps of Jesus. So, I guess I'm just one of those crazy Christians! |
| MRS. BEA: | You'd let people throw rocks at you, just to prove you are a Christian? |
| MRS. MUNK: | I'm not sure I have that much courage. I hope I'd never deny my faith. I know my faith is important . . . it's changed my life. And if the kids will help me, I'll pray for the courage to be a Christian in a tough world. |

**Have Mrs. Munk pray this prayer with the children:**
Dear God, I really hope I won't have to suffer like Stephen. I'm not sure I have his courage. But if my faith is tested, please stay close to me and give me the strength and the courage I might need. Amen.

# REV. PUGGINS HEARS THE RUMOR

## Characters:

Mrs. Munk

Rev. Puggins

**LEADER:** Just last week old Grumpy went huffing and puffing down to Mrs. Munk's home in the middle of the night. He said he had gotten some voice mail that said, "Tell Grumpy that Grandpa is coming." He was so excited, he just had to tell someone; so he hurried down to Mrs. Munk's. Now she has gotten excited . . . and, well . . . here she goes:

(*REV. PUGGINS has his head down and is snoring.*)

**MRS. MUNK:** Oh, Rev. Puggins. Wake up, Rev. Puggins! It's me, Mrs. Munk.

**REV. PUGGINS:** Oh, hi, Mrs. Munk. What brings you out on this fine day?

**MRS. MUNK:** I just had to share something I heard.

**REV. PUGGINS:** Oh, please be careful now, if it's a rumor. You know, rumors are like soft butter, very easy to spread. But, oh, so hard to unspread.

**MRS. MUNK:** I don't think this is just a rumor . . . and it's not anything bad at all.

**REV. PUGGINS:** Oh, in that case, I suppose it's okay.

**MRS. MUNK:** Grumpy got some voice mail and —

**REV. PUGGINS:** (*Interrupting*) I didn't know Grumpy had one of those gadgets.

**MRS. MUNK:** No, he doesn't. This is real voice mail. It came from one of his distant cousins way down south. It's that thing they do on the phone!

**REV. PUGGINS:** I never thought about telephoning as voice mail, but I guess —

**MRS. MUNK:** (*Interrupting*) Anyway, this cousin called and said, "Tell Grumpy that Grandpa is coming."

**REV. PUGGINS:** Are you sure?

**MRS. MUNK:** Just as sure as I'm standing here. Grumpy was so excited, why, he was about to bust!

**REV. PUGGINS:** I can imagine. I've certainly missed Grandpa, and Tee too. I wonder if Tee is coming? You know they left together.

**MRS. MUNK:** I hope so. I always liked his hairdo.

**REV. PUGGINS:** I'm not so sure about his hairdo, but your feet are surely beautiful today, Mrs. Munk. Yes ma'am, beautiful indeed!

(*Mrs. Munk looks at her feet.*)

MRS. MUNK:  Beautiful? I don't think so . . . same old feet!

REV. PUGGINS:  Well, Isaiah says, "How beautiful upon the mountain are the feet of those who bring good news," and you have really brought news that brightens up this day! What a wonderful thought! I think that idea deserves a nice prayer. Help me, boys and girls.


**Have Rev. Puggins pray this prayer with the children:**
Dear God, help us to remember to thank you when we hear good news. Help us to remember people who are far away from us, because you are with us wherever we go. Amen.

# REV. PUGGINS CHECKS OUT THE RUMOR

### Character:
Rev. Puggins

### Production Note:
*After the introduction, you will need to get a member
of the congregation to come down to the stage area
so you can talk to him or her. If no one is available,
you'll have to talk to the pastor, but that is not a good choice.
Tell the audience member ahead of time the questions
you will be asking him or her to answer.*


LEADER:　A couple of weeks ago, Grumpy got some wonderful news from a cousin way down south. The message came by voice mail and said, "Tell Grumpy that Grandpa is coming." Word spread quickly through Harmony, and Mrs. Munk told Rev. Puggins. Rev. Puggins was never one to believe rumors or gossip, so he decided to check it out himself.

REV. PUGGINS:　Well, let's see. How do I do this?

(*Pause while* REV. PUGGINS *thinks for awhile.*)

REV. PUGGINS:　Hmmm. Hmmm. I guess I could write Grandpa a note. We have his address in the office.

REV. PUGGINS:　Naaah! That would take too long. I could use the Internet, but my computer is acting up.

*(Pause again while Rev. Puggins thinks for awhile.)*

Rev. Puggins:  Hmmm. Hmmm. I've got it! At least I think I have it!

Rev. Puggins:  Ummm. If I remember right, Grandpa was going to live at a nice place called the Truesdale's Golden Dream Retirement Center. I think that's the place. And I think some of the folks right here might have some sort of connection to the people who run that retirement center!

Rev. Puggins:  Anybody here know a family named Truesdale? If you have talked or written to any Truesdale in the past couple of weeks, would you stand up so I can see you? Please stand tall. I had to leave my pulpit, and I can't see very well from here.

*(Plan for the audience member to stand at this time.)*

Rev. Puggins:  Okay, it looks like we have a real live person who has talked to a Truesdale lately. Would you come down for a few moments and take the microphone?

Rev. Puggins:  Would you give your first name . . . er, just for the record?

*(Have the audience member give his or her first name.)*

Rev. Puggins:  And when, would you say, that you last talked to one of those Truesdales?

*(Have the audience member respond with an answer such as, "Recently," or "Just last week.")*

REV. PUGGINS:   Could I ask what you talked about? Ummm, if it was private, never mind . . . but maybe it could help me clear up a rumor. Did any of the Truesdales mention that Grandpa might be moving back? Was that part of it?

(*Have the audience member respond with an answer such as "Yes, they said that Grandpa is moving back.")*

REV. PUGGINS:   Were any dates mentioned?

(*Have the audience member respond with an answer such as, "They didn't know" or "Very soon."*

REV. PUGGINS:   Uh huh . . . well! It looks that the rumor is more than a rumor, and the voice mail Grumpy heard was right!! Yeeehaw! My friend Grandpa is coming back!

(*Have the audience member return to his or her seat.*)

REV. PUGGINS:   If I can get some help, I'd like to thank God for all God's blessings, especially this one!


**Have Rev. Puggins pray this prayer with the children:**
Dear God, thanks for friends, wherever they are; they make our lives richer. And thanks for good news. Amen.

# GRANDPA, HOME AT LAST!

## Characters:
Grumpy
Grandpa
Mrs. Munk

**LEADER:** Grumpy had gone way out to the edge of Harmony. He told everyone that he just wanted to stretch his legs, but he had something else in mind too. He found a high place in the path where he could look far away. He wanted to be the first to see Grandpa return! But the sun was warm, and after a while Grumpy grew drowsy.

(*Have* GRUMPY *make snoring noises.*)

**GRANDPA:** Well, hello, friend Grumpy.

(*Have* GRUMPY *continue to make snoring noises.*)

**GRANDPA:** (*Louder*) I said, "Hello, friend Grumpy!"

(GRUMPY *wakes up and rubs his eyes.*)

**GRUMPY:** Hello. Why, it's — *Harumph!* — Grandpa! Hi, Grandpa!

(GRUMPY *is talking nonstop.*)

GRUMPY: How are you? Gosh, I've missed you! Where have you been? What have you been doing? Are you well now? What did you — *Harumph!* — see in your travels? Have you — *Harumph!* — seen Mrs. Munk yet? She really misses you. *Harumph! Harumph!* Excuse the *harumphs*; it's just that I'm excited.

GRANDPA: I'm excited too, Grumpy! I just show it in different ways! We've got lots of time to talk about where I've been and what I've done. Right now I'd just like to see some of my old friends. Is that Mrs. Munk I see down the trail there?

GRUMPY: Yep! That's Mrs. Munk. She's been a big help to me while you were gone!

(*MRS. MUNK has her back to GRUMPY and GRANDPA. GRANDPA shouts to get her attention.*)

GRANDPA: Hi, Mrs. Munk! I'm home! I'm home at last!

(*MRS. MUNK turns around fast.*)

MRS. MUNK: I can't believe it! Good gracious! Heavenly days! My stars! It really is you! Grandpa, could I give you a little welcome home hug?

GRANDPA: Sure! I can always use a nice hug.

(*GRANDPA and MRS. MUNK hug.*)

GRUMPY: *Harumph!* I think I'm missing something.

GRANDPA &
MRS. MUNK: What, Grumpy?

**105**

GRUMPY:     I think I miss getting hugged! Harumph! Do you think it's because I *harumph* so much? Is that why people don't hug me?

GRANDPA:    Might be, Grumpy! I didn't look for cactus plants to hug when I was in the dessert. Cactus plants just don't look friendly. Maybe if you looked friendlier, folks would hug you like they do Mrs. Munk.

GRUMPY:     I'd like that! I might act tough, but I want to be loved.

MRS. MUNK:  Well, Grumpy let me be the first.

(*MRS. MUNK hugs GRUMPY.*)

GRANDPA:    And I'll be the second.

(*GRANDPA hugs GRUMPY.*)

GRANDPA:    Now let's have a prayer, led by our pastor.


**Lead the children in a prayer.**

# HI THERE, MR. RATCHET!

### Characters:
Mr. Ratchet
Grandpa

LEADER: Mr. Ratchet has been about to bust his britches since he heard that Grandpa is coming back. He watched the path for hours, but finally was worn out and has laid down to rest.

(*MR. RATCHET is sleeping and snoring. GRANDPA approaches and holds his finger to his mouth.*)

GRANDPA: Sshhh . . . let's wait a moment.

(*GRANDPA walks right up to MR. RATCHET's ear.*)

GRANDPA: Hi there, Mr. Ratchet!

(*MR. RATCHET is still sleeping, talking, and snoring, all at the same time.*)

MR. RATCHET: Zzzz. Hello, Grandpa. Hello there, Grandpa. Zzzz. Grandpa is coming. Zzzz.

(*GRANDPA nudges MR. RATCHET.*)

GRANDPA: Wake up, sleepy head! I'm home!

(*MR. RATCHET's head pops up. He turns toward Grandpa.*)

| | |
|---|---|
| **MR. RATCHET:** | Grandpa! (*Gives* GRANDPA *a big hug.*) It really is you! I'm not dreaming! |
| **GRANDPA:** | Nope, you aren't dreaming. I'm really here. And I'm here to stay! |
| **MR. RATCHET:** | You won't be running off again? |
| **GRANDPA:** | Nope, didn't much care for the Truesdale Golden Retirement Center. Oh, it was a nice place and all that, but this . . . this is home. |
| **MR. RATCHET:** | How was your trip? Somebody said you were flying in. |
| **GRANDPA:** | Two words describe that trip . . . long and bumpy! And it got a little stuffy in that airplane. I had to share one seat with Tee, Cleo, and Dandee. I think Tee got excited when the plane took off. He closed his eyes, was breathing hard, and about used up all our air. I really wanted to ride in the car, look out the window and all, but the fellow who runs the retirement center thought we'd be just fine in that airplane. What does he know? |
| **MR. RATCHET:** | You mentioned Tee, Cleo, and Dandee. Did they come along? Where are they? |
| **GRANDPA:** | Yep. They came along in the same airplane, same seat! I think they are back at the house resting up. But I had to come up to your house. I wanted to say hello to my good friend, Mr. Ratchet. |
| **MR. RATCHET:** | I'm sure glad to see you. Welcome home, Grandpa! I've been trying to keep things going while you were away. |

GRANDPA: So you have been going to church, reading your Bible, and saying your prayers?

MR. RATCHET: I don't read so well, Grandpa. But I'm a pretty good listener.

GRANDPA: Do you remember how to lead a prayer? How about a prayer?

MR. RATCHET: Sure, if the kids will help. Okay, kids? Here goes.

**Have Mr. Ratchet pray this prayer with the children:**
Dear God, this is Mr. Ratchet, asking you to bless all the people who make our world such a nice place. Give them your love, God . . . We'll give them our love too. Amen.

# TEE RETURNS

### Characters:
Grumpy
Tee

| | |
|---|---|
| LEADER: | Grumpy came down from his hilltop to visit Mrs. Munk. But the first critter he saw as he entered Harmony was this boy with the funny haircut, the one everybody calls Tee. |
| GRUMPY: | Well — *Harumph!* — It looks like the old Tee-bone is back in town! |
| TEE: | Hi, Grumpy. |
| GRUMPY: | Heard you came back, riding in first class. |
| TEE: | I wouldn't say that. There were five of us in one seat! Grandpa got excited when we got on the plane, got real excited, and started breathing funny, just about used up all our air! Nope, we weren't in first class . . . maybe worst class . . . but not first class! |
| GRUMPY: | Funny. *Harumph!* Grandpa has a different story about the trip. |
| TEE: | Well, you know how people get when they are old . . . they forget things. |

| | |
|---|---|
| GRUMPY: | He seemed to remember pretty well, and he said that you are the one who was — *Harumph!* — breathing funny. |
| TEE: | Well, maybe I did get a little upset. |
| GRUMPY: | *Harumph!* Grandpa said you kept your eyes closed at takeoff. |
| TEE: | Well, maybe for awhile . . . |
| GRUMPY: | So, why blame Grandpa? |
| TEE: | Ummm . . . he's handy, and he was there! |
| GRUMPY: | I guess that's why Adam blamed Eve when he ate the apple. *Harumph!* She was handy, and she was there too! |
| TEE: | I guess I shouldn't have done that. |
| GRUMPY: | I — Harumph! — guess not. And especially with me! I think Grandpa is one terrific fellow. |
| TEE: | But it's so hard to admit it when you do something like that. |
| GRUMPY: | Sure it is. But Grandpa once told me — *Harumph!* — that when I matured as a Christian, I'd — *Harumph!* — stop blaming other people when I messed up. |
| TEE: | So you are saying — |

| GRUMPY: | I'm saying — *Harumph!* — grow up, Tee! You've been around long enough to know better. |
| TEE: | Yeah, I guess so. |
| GRUMPY: | I'm going to pray for you, Tee. And I'm going to ask the kids to help. |

**Have Grumpy pray this prayer with the children:**
Dear God, this is — *Harumph!* — Grumpy again. I'm praying for all folks who blame other people for the messes they make. Bless them, Lord. Help us to always admit the things we have done wrong and to ask for forgiveness. Amen.

# SOMEONE BORROWED TEE'S SOFTBALL

### Characters:
Tee
Grandpa

**LEADER:** Grandpa and Tee had made their move back to Harmony without any problems. They were just getting settled when Tee made a disturbing discovery.

**TEE:** Hey, Grandpa!

**GRANDPA:** Yes, Tee?

**TEE:** You been playing with my softball, Grandpa?

**GRANDPA:** Well, forty years ago I might have been a pretty good shortstop in a softball game, but those times are long gone. I haven't seen your softball, Tee. Are you sure it came with us? Sometimes things get lost when we move around.

**TEE:** I'm pretty sure it made the move, Grandpa! I was playing catch with Dandee on Saturday!

**GRANDPA:** Where were you and Dandee playing catch?

**TEE:** Out front. You won't let us throw the ball in the house.

**GRANDPA:** Hmmm. And you have looked all over your room?

| | |
|---|---|
| **TEE:** | I've looked in my room, your room, the living room. I've even searched the bathroom . . . the front yard . . . no softball. And it was pretty special to me. |
| **GRANDPA:** | You didn't loan it to anyone? |
| **TEE:** | No! I'd never loan it. It's the one you gave me . . . remember? |
| **GRANDPA:** | Oh, yes, your birthday. Sure, I remember. |
| **TEE:** | Grandpa, you don't think anyone would steal my softball, do you? |
| **GRANDPA:** | I don't like to think that there are such people, but I'm afraid they really do exist, Tee. Some would steal, and some might even hurt you if you had something they wanted. |
| **TEE:** | I guess I'll just tell everybody to keep his or her eyes open. Maybe my ball will show up. I sure hope so. |
| **GRANDPA:** | I hope so, too, Tee. And I hope it is just missing or borrowed and not stolen. I hope we don't have those kind of people around here. |
| **TEE:** | Would it be okay if we prayed and asked God to help? |
| **GRANDPA:** | It's always okay to ask God's help. And I'd like our friends to help too. |

**Have Grandpa pray this prayer with the children:**
Dear God, we know you want what is good for all your children. Remind us that we can come to you in prayer for help with any problem, no matter how small or how big. Thank you, God. Amen.

# A QUIET DAY IN HARMONY

### Characters:
Grumpy
Grandpa

**LEADER:** It was the middle of summer, and it was very hot in Harmony. It seemed as though everything had slowed down. We find Grandpa and Grumpy talking about what has been happening — or not happening — in Harmony.

**GRUMPY:** *Harumph!* Gosh, Grandpa, it's getting B-O-R-I-N-G around here! Nothing is going on . . .nothing happening at all!

**GRANDPA:** Well, the fair just pulled into town, and soon there will be bright lights and rides. But you are right. After weeks of excitement, it has been very quiet in Harmony.

**GRUMPY:** No babies born . . . no barn fires . . . no dumb ol' visitors . . . no nothing!

**GRANDPA:** Isn't it wonderful?

**GRUMPY:** *Harumph!* What? I like a little excitement! I was just thinking about chasing the neighbor kids out of my yard . . . not much, just enough to get them scared.

| GRANDPA: | But Grumpy, excitement usually means that someone is getting hurt. I don't like to hear sirens. They might mean there is a fire or a wreck. I really don't like to hear the helicopter leaving our hospital. That means somebody is really, really sick. I like ordinary days without excitement. |
|---|---|
| GRUMPY: | I — *Harumph!* — guess I see what you mean. |
| GRANDPA: | We need the quiet times, Grumpy. We need to be refreshed so we can handle the tough times. I think that is what the Sabbath is all about, but you might check with Rev. Puggins on that. |
| GRUMPY: | I'll take your word on that, Grandpa. Old Rev. Puggins would probably want to preach me a little sermon, and I'm in no mood . . . |
| GRANDPA: | I don't think so, Grumpy. He has to have his own quiet times just like we do. Once he said his "cup was almost empty," and that's bad. He needed time alone. |
| GRUMPY: | Why didn't he just — *Harumph!* — dip his dumb ol' cup in the creek? |
| GRANDPA: | Oh, Grumpy, you still don't understand. Rev. Puggins was saying that he was stressed out . . . that he needed a rest . . . a Sabbath. That's what he meant. |
| GRUMPY: | Oh. Don't tell him what I said about his . . . uh . . . cup and the creek. |

GRANDPA: Of course I wouldn't do that! But if these boys and girls will help, we'll have a prayer thanking God for these boring, quiet days. Will you, boys and girls?

**Have Grandpa pray this prayer with the children:**
Dear God, it is so nice to be bored when nobody is getting hurt, no barns are burning, and our spirits are refreshed. Thank you, God, for quiet days. Amen.

# WHOSE SOFTBALL IS THAT?

## Characters:
Mrs. Bea
Mrs. Munk

**LEADER:** A couple of weeks ago, Tee asked Grandpa if he had seen his softball. It was the one Grandpa had given Tee for his birthday, so it was pretty special. Tee searched high and low, but no softball.

(*MRS. BEA is tossing a softball and catching it. She misses a catch.*)

**MRS. BEA:** I need a little help, boys and girls!

(*Call a child by name; have him or her return the softball.*)

**MRS. BEA:** Thanks!

(*MRS. BEA is almost ready to start throwing again, when MRS. MUNK arrives.*)

**MRS. BEA:** Well, hi there, Mrs. Munk!

**MRS. MUNK:** Hello, Mrs. Bea, how are you today?

**MRS. BEA:** I'm just fine . . . playing a little catch. You any good at playing catch, Mrs. Munk?

| | |
|---|---|
| MRS. MUNK: | I played left field for the Harmony Scramblers team last year. I guess I can catch pretty well. But where did you get that softball? |
| MRS. BEA: | This old ball? I found it. |
| MRS. MUNK: | Found it? |
| MRS. BEA: | Sure! I guess somebody threw it away . . . and I found it. |
| MRS. MUNK: | Could I ask where you found it? |
| MRS. BEA: | Why? It's my ball. I found it. |
| MRS. MUNK: | Well, Tee lost a special softball. It was one that Grandpa had given him . . . and Grandpa had written something special on it. |

(MRS. BEA *looks at the softball.*)

| | |
|---|---|
| MRS. BEA: | And what did the old geezer write? |
| MRS. MUNK: | He wrote "hit one over the fence for me" on the cover. |

(MRS. BEA *moves the softball out of* MRS. MUNK'S *sight.*)

| | |
|---|---|
| MRS. BEA: | That's nice. |
| MRS. MUNK: | Well, throw it here, I'll show you how I can catch. |
| MRS. BEA: | I've changed my mind. I guess I'll be going home now. |
| MRS. MUNK: | Okay, but could I take a look at the ball? |

MRS. BEA:     Sorry. I'm late, gotta run. Bye!

(*MRS. BEA hurries off stage.*)

MRS. MUNK:    Hmmm. I sure do wonder where she got that
              softball. What do you think, boys and girls? Did
              any of you get a look at the ball? Is Mrs. Bea
              fibbing and trying to keep Tee's ball?

(*Let the children respond to the questions.*)

MRS. MUNK:    Ooooh . . . I think this needs some prayer! Help
              me now.

**Have Mrs. Munk pray this prayer with the children:**
Dear God, things are not always what they seem. When our
friends are hurt, show us how to help them. Amen.

# A LETTER

**<u>Character:</u>**
Mrs. Munk

Mrs. Munk
Harmony Lane
Harmony

To The Boys and Girls
Of Our Church

Dear Boys and Girls,

I haven't ever written you before, but I need some help. Tee is really upset about losing his softball. I don't think we'll ever get it back. I think it is under somebody's bed right now.

I saw Tee crying yesterday, and it just broke my heart. So I got to thinking that maybe Tee's friends could buy him another softball. That is why I need your help. We Munks don't have much money. I might get a little bit selling bread, but it won't be enough to buy a softball. If any of you have an extra penny, we could put them all together . . . then we might have enough for a new softball.

If you can help, I'd sure appreciate it; and I know Tee would be thankful.

Sincerely,

Mrs. Munk

*After reading the letter, the pastor or leader might talk to the children about a real need in the community and end with a prayer for God's help in helping others.*

# MRS. MUNK: CHRISTIAN IN ACTION

## Characters:
Mrs. Munk
Boys
Girls

## Production Notes:
*The children will need to have copies of the script
and be prepped to respond.*

| | |
|---|---|
| LEADER: | Tee, Grandpa, and Mrs. Munk looked all over Grandpa's yard. But no softball! Tee was really heartbroken at the loss. He didn't know when he could get another ball. But Mrs. Munk has an idea. |
| MRS. MUNK: | Hi, boys and girls. |
| BOYS & GIRLS: | Hi, Mrs. Munk! |
| MRS. MUNK: | Were you able to . . . ? |
| GIRL: | We did what you suggested, Mrs. Munk. |
| MRS. MUNK: | You took up a little love offering for Tee? To buy Tee a new ball?? |

| | |
|---|---|
| BOY: | Yep, that's what we did. |
| MRS. MUNK: | Did you folks have enough for a ball? |
| GIRL: | Almost enough. We might be just a little short. |
| MRS. MUNK: | Well, I sold some of my homemade bread to the Smith family, and maybe with that we will have enough. |
| BOY: | I hope so. |
| GIRL: | Will you buy the ball? We don't know our way around Harmony. You'd know where the store is, wouldn't you? |
| MRS. MUNK: | Sure, I'd be glad to buy the ball. |
| BOY: | I hope you can get to the store this week. Tee really misses that ball! |
| MRS. MUNK: | Hmmm. I wonder if we should get Grandpa to write on it, like he did on the other one? Maybe not. That way we'd be trying to fool Tee into thinking this was the first ball. Instead, let's get Grandpa to sign it after we give it to Tee. |
| BOYS & GIRLS: | Sure! — that'll work — yeah! |
| MRS. MUNK: | Now I'd like to thank you for helping with this. If there is any money left over, I'll put it on the altar, and the church can use it to help some other people. |

**Boys & Girls:** That sounds good! Let's do it!

**Mrs. Munk:** But for right now, let's talk to God, okay?

**Have Mrs. Munk pray this prayer with the children:**
Dear God, we know it is better to give than to receive. Help us always remember that. Bless all our friends here at church and all your children everywhere. Amen.

*If you have raised money for a special project, thank the children and their families for their contributions.*

# A NEW SOFTBALL FOR TEE

### Characters:
Tee

Mrs. Munk

**LEADER:** Two weeks ago Mrs. Munk asked our boys and girls to help her buy a new softball for Tee. With their money and the money she got from selling bread, there was just enough to buy the new ball. On the way home, Mrs. Munk saw Tee heading toward the same store.

**TEE:** Oh, hi, Mrs. Munk . . . haven't seen you in a coon's age! (*Giggle*)

**MRS. MUNK:** You've been running around with Grumpy again, haven't you? That is his favorite saying.

**TEE:** Yeah, I guess I have been spending time with Grumpy. Been to the store, Mrs. Munk?

**MRS. MUNK:** Yes. I had a little shopping to do. You'd probably like to know about my shopping trip.

**TEE:** Not really. I'm going for a double scoop of ice cream. That's about all the shopping I'm really interested in on a hot day.

**MRS. MUNK:** Nothing else at all would interest you?

| | |
|---|---|
| TEE: | Well, sure . . . I guess I'd be interested in skateboards or video games or . . . or a softball. But I know you won't be buying any of those things. |
| MRS. MUNK: | You might be surprised, Tee. |
| TEE: | (*Interested; excited*) What do you mean? What did you buy? |
| MRS. MUNK: | Well, I sure didn't have enough money for a skateboard or a video game . . . but I did have enough for a new softball. It's right here in my shopping bag. |
| TEE: | Wow! Can I play with it sometime? |
| MRS. MUNK: | You can play with it all the time. It's yours! |
| TEE: | Mine? Really mine? But how did you . . . ? You don't have much money . . . so how? |
| MRS. MUNK: | I had help. You have lots of friends, Tee. Some are the boys and girls right there in front of us . . . they each contributed a little bit. Then I sold a few loaves of homemade bread . . . and it was just enough! |
| TEE: | You bought me a ball! I can't believe it! A new softball . . . Yeeehaww! |
| MRS. MUNK: | There are two rules that come with this ball, Tee. Rule number one is . . . have fun with your new ball. That should be easy enough. Rule number two is . . . take care of your new ball. Okay? |

TEE:   Sure . . . no problem! But, gosh . . . I don't know how to thank you. It's like a dream that has come true! Can I say a little prayer about my friends? Can I?

**Have Tee pray this prayer with the children:**
Dear God, friends are so very special. They laugh with you, and they cry with you. And they find ways to show their love. Thank you, God, for friends. Amen.

# MRS. BEA SUFFERS A LOSS

### Characters:
Mrs. Bea
Mrs. Munk

### Production Notes:
*Mrs. Bea is not wearing her apron.*

LEADER: Tee has already hit a home run with his new softball, and Grandpa was there to watch it happen! It looked like things had settled down in the village, until Mrs. Bea showed up at Mrs. Munk's door.

MRS. BEA: Hellooo, Mrs. Munk! Are you there, Mrs. Munk? I really need to see you.

(*MRS. MUNK comes upstairs to the stage.*)

MRS. MUNK: Oh! Good morning, Mrs. Bea. It's a lovely day today. Isn't it?

MRS. BEA: It was lovely. It was lovely until I went outside this morning!

MRS. MUNK: Why, what in the world would have changed it so fast?

| | |
|---|---|
| MRS. BEA: | I'll tell you what . . . it's gone! Vanished . . . probably some prankster. Or maybe a thief. But it's gone, and now I feel all . . . exposed! |
| MRS. MUNK: | What's gone? What thief? |
| MRS. BEA: | Are you telling me that you didn't notice? My apron . . . it's gone! |
| MRS. MUNK: | Oh, so it is! I never had much use for aprons myself. |
| MRS. BEA: | Have you ever seen me without that apron? Now it's gone, and I just know that one of those young hoodlums — maybe Tee — has got it! |
| MRS. MUNK: | Whoa, now! Tee is a good boy. I don't think he'd be involved in stealing your apron. It's not like him at all. Why don't you try to remember exactly where you hung it? Maybe it's just lost. |
| MRS. BEA: | I washed it out after dinner last night. Then I took it outside my lodge and hung it on that maple sapling near the creek bank. I'm sure I hung it there, because I could reach the lower limbs when the wind was blowing. |
| MRS. MUNK: | Lots of wind last night, huh? |
| MRS. BEA: | You didn't hear the storm? I guess you don't hear those things in your home under the oak tree. But I sure heard it! It was a real frog strangler! |
| MRS. MUNK: | Let's see, you hung the apron on a sapling near the creek bank, and the wind was whipping it around, right? |

| | |
|---|---|
| MRS. BEA: | Right! |
| MRS. MUNK: | And there was a storm, with even more wind. And this morning the apron is gone, right? |
| MRS. BEA: | Right again . . . so what? |
| MRS. MUNK: | Have you thought that the wind might be your "thief?" Have you thought it might have just blown away? It might be caught in a tree somewhere, or hung on a bush. |
| MRS. BEA: | Well, I never. That is a possibility! Maybe some of these folks around here would help me search . . . if you are sure it wasn't that Tee character? |
| MRS. MUNK: | I'd be glad to help organize a search, and I'd be glad to ask God to help too. |

**Have Mrs. Munk pray this prayer with the children:**
Dear God, sometimes we lose something we treasure. Remind us to look closely at where we have been during the day. Thank you for being there when we call on you. When our treasures are found, may we always remember to give you our thanks and praise. Amen.

# SEARCHING, SEARCHING, SEARCHING

**Characters:**
Rev. Puggins
Tee


LEADER: Mrs. Bea's apron has mysteriously vanished. She draped it across a small sapling as a storm hit the village. Now it's gone. Her first thought was that Tee had taken the apron. Mrs. Munk assured her that Tee would do no such thing. The entire community turned out to search. Let's join a couple of them.

REV. PUGGINS: I looked all the way up to the hilltop, Tee. Where did you look?

TEE: I started at Mrs. Bea's place. But when I got there, she came out and just stood there and glared at me. I don't think she likes me.

REV. PUGGINS: Ah, come on, Tee. Everybody likes you!

TEE: Maybe everybody . . . but Mrs. Bea!

REV. PUGGINS: You really think she doesn't like you?

TEE: I really do.

REV. PUGGINS: And yet you are out here in the hot sun, trying to find her apron. Tee, that's such a nice thing to do!

TEE: Oh, you mean hunting like I'm doing?

REV. PUGGINS: No, I mean finding enough love in your heart to help someone who might not even like you at all. Reminds me of a sermon I preached on the good Samaritan. Would you like to hear the main points?

TEE: Ummm . . . I think I hear Grandpa calling me for lunch. Maybe another time? There is one story that might help us right now. I think it's about a woman who lost something.

REV. PUGGINS: Why, sure! It's in Luke. And it tells of a woman who had ten coins, then loses one of them. It describes how very carefully she sweeps her house and lights a lamp to find what she has lost. Does that give you any ideas, Tee?

TEE: Yes, sir! That gives me the idea that we could get all our folks together and sweep through the woods near Mrs. Bea's place. That's a great idea. Thanks, Rev. Puggins!

REV. PUGGINS: I'm afraid it wasn't my idea, Tee. I was quoting Luke. Luke was quoting Jesus. If this works, we should thank Jesus.

TEE: I just know it'll work! We'll sweep through the woods like a big broom! If the apron is there, we are sure to find it. If you'll lead the kids in a prayer, I'll go find more folks to join our search. We could call it Operation Big Broom!

(*TEE leaves the stage.*)

REV. PUGGINS: I wish Tee had stayed for the prayer. We all need prayer, but sometimes we seem too busy to stop and pray.

**Have Rev. Puggins pray this prayer with the children:**
Dear God, when we are searching, remind us to search every high place and every low place. We ask for your help. We thank you for the help you have already given in our Scriptures. Amen.

# TEE'S VISIT TO MRS. BEA

### Characters:
Tee
Mrs. Bea

**LEADER:** Tee organized what he called "Operation Big Broom" to sweep through the woods around Mrs. Bea's house. He is now reporting back to Mrs. Bea.

(*TEE knocks on MRS. BEA's door.*)

**TEE:** Yoo hoo! Mrs. Bea, are you home?

(*MRS. BEA is out of sight.*)

**MRS. BEA:** Yes . . . yes, I am. What is it?

**TEE:** I just came by to give you a report, Mrs. Bea.

**MRS. BEA:** Well, just a minute while I close a window.

(*MRS. BEA comes upstairs to the stage.*)

**MRS. BEA:** Didn't find it, did you?

**TEE:** Well, no, I didn't find it.

| | |
|---|---|
| Mrs. Bea: | I still think somebody took it. Maybe it was that Grumpy. Some folks just don't respect other people's property. Yep, I bet it was Grumpy! |
| Tee: | I said, "I didn't find it," and I didn't! Grumpy was the one who found it! |

(*Tee holds out the apron.*)

| | |
|---|---|
| Tee: | It was about half a mile from your home. |
| Mrs. Bea: | Well, bless my soul! And that's it you have? Oh my, you would not believe how happy this makes me. Young folks, why, they are so thoughtful! Would you tell him that I'll . . . I'll make him a nice cake? |
| Tee: | He'd like that. |
| Mrs. Bea: | And you returned it for Mr. Grumpy? |
| Tee: | Grumpy would have brought it to you, but he had to run an errand for Grandpa. |
| Mrs. Bea: | You knew how much I missed it, so you made a special trip to bring it back. |
| Tee: | Yes ma'am. I lost something once. It was very special to me. I know exactly how it feels to lose something. I sure do. |
| Mrs. Bea: | And you helped organize the search party? Somebody told me you named it "Operation Big Broom." |

| TEE: | That's right. Nearly all the folks from Harmony helped. The little guys looked under bushes, the taller ones looked in trees. The Munksters were there. Even Rev. Puggins gave up his afternoon nap to help. |
|---|---|
| MRS. BEA: | Well, you just don't have any idea how happy this makes me! Thank you. Thank you. Thank you. |
| TEE: | We were about to give up, but I think Grumpy had some extra help. He just kept on going until he found it. Rev. Puggins said that maybe God was leading him to the apron. He did ask God to help, you know. |
| MRS. BEA: | Yes, I heard that. I suppose we should give God a word of thanks. But I need a little help from the boys and girls. |

**Have Mrs. Bea pray this prayer with the children:**
Dear God, I've got some strange feelings in my heart. One of them ????

# MRS. BEA HAS A DILEMMA

### Characters:
Mrs. Bea
Mrs. Munk

**LEADER:** A long time ago, the Hebrews received a set of laws. We call them the mosaic laws because they came from God through Moses. One of those laws mentions "bearing false witness." Another mentions "stealing." Now, Mrs. Bea still has Tee's softball hidden away under her bed and has accused both Tee and Grumpy of taking her apron. She doesn't really know the Ten Commandments, but she's beginning to think she has done something wrong.

**MRS. BEA:** Oh, Mrs. Munk. Are you in, Mrs. Munk?

(*MRS. MUNK is out of sight.*)

**MRS. MUNK:** Yes, I'm here, Mrs. Bea. Just a moment. I'll be right out.

(*Pause while MRS. MUNK finishes whatever she is doing. Then MRS. MUNK comes on stage.*)

**MRS. MUNK:** Whew! It's laundry day at the Munk home. I didn't know the little Munksters could get that many clothes dirty! How are you on this fine day, Mrs. Bea?

| | |
|---|---|
| MRS. BEA: | Ummm, I guess I'm okay. But I have a couple of questions, and I didn't know whom else to ask. |
| MRS. MUNK: | No problem! The laundry can wait. Fire away. |
| MRS. BEA: | It's really just hypo . . . hypothet . . . oh, what is that word? |
| MRS. MUNK: | Is the word you are looking for *hypothetical*? It's a big fifty-cent word that means imaginary, like an imaginary situation. |
| MRS. BEA: | That's the word! Now just suppose — this is purely hypothetical, of course — just suppose that you wanted something that belonged to somebody else. Then you found a way to get it, and you had it hidden under your bed . . . hypothetically, of course. What would you do? |
| MRS. MUNK: | That's easy enough. I'd give it back. |
| MRS. BEA: | But what if . . . what if you had told somebody that you didn't have this hypothetical thing? |
| MRS. MUNK: | Then I'd say that your hypothetical person might be not only a thief, but a liar as well! |
| MRS. BEA: | And what if that hypothetical person accused other folks of stealing something very precious, but they didn't? And the ones who were accused worked the hardest to find the missing apron . . . er . . . thing. Hypothetically speaking, of course. |

| | |
|---|---|
| MRS. MUNK: | I'd say that hypothetical person is making a pretty good start on breaking the Ten Commandments. And I thought I was the only one with dirty linens! |
| MRS. BEA: | Hmmm. I'll pass all that along to the hypothetical person. |
| MRS. MUNK: | And maybe you should pray for that person too. |
| MRS. BEA: | Ummm. I'd feel a little uncomfortable. I'm pretty close to that person, . . . but okay. Boys and girls, help me now. |

**Have Mrs. Bea pray this prayer with the children:**
Dear God . . . what in the world . . . should that . . . hyp-o-thet-ical person do now? Please guide me . . . ummm, her. In Jesus' name. Amen.

# SOFTBALL RETURNED - A NEW FRIENDSHIP IN HARMONY

### Characters:
Mrs. Bea
Grumpy
Tee

**LEADER:** Things were settling down in Harmony. Tee and Grumpy had become neighborhood heroes for finding and returning Mrs. Bea's apron. And Mrs. Bea had done a lot of thinking since that day. We find her today looking for Tee.

**MRS. BEA:** Oh . . .. Uh, excuse me, Mr. Grumpy. Have you seen Tee?

**GRUMPY:** *Harumph!* I think he's just down the path, Mrs. Bea. I'd go along with you, but I've got some errands. Sometimes I feel like a gopher instead of a person! Go fer this . . . go fer that.

**MRS. BEA:** Well, gophers are not so bad. In fact, I think they are cute.

**GRUMPY:** Well, yeah, I guess so. Anyway, see you later. I've got my errands. Tell ol' Tee-bone I said, "hi."

(*GRUMPY leaves the stage. MRS. BEA moves about halfway across the stage.*)

MRS. BEA:    Oh, Tee! Tee, are you here? Tee?

(*MRS. BEA looks away from TEE's location. TEE pops up to the stage.*)

TEE:    Here I am, over here, Mrs. Bea.

(*MRS. BEA turns toward TEE.*)

MRS. BEA:    Oh, yes, there you are.

TEE:    Were you looking for me?

MRS. BEA:    Yes, I was, Tee. I've got a serious question that I must ask you.

TEE:    Whatever it was, I didn't do it . . . honest!

MRS. BEA:    No, no . . . not that kind of question. My question is . . . well, it's . . . ummm . . . the question . . . I'm having some trouble with this, Tee, so I'll just say it out loud.

(*MRS. BEA begins talking very fast in a mumbling voice.*)

MRS. BEA:    Could you forgive a lady who found your softball, hid it for a while, but is ready to give it back now?

TEE:    Whaaat? You'll have to slow down a bit. I heard something about forgive and softball. The rest was kind of shoved all together.

MRS. BEA:     Okay. It shouldn't be as hard this time. Tee, I found your softball out in the yard. I took it and hid it under my bed. I wanted it. I didn't think it was a big deal until I lost my apron. Then you returned my apron! It made me want to cry! I couldn't sleep in my bed another night with the ball under there. I just had to return it to you. So, here it is. Can you forgive a lady who made a mistake? Huh . . . can you, Tee?

TEE:     Well, golly, it's the ball that Grandpa wrote on, "Hit one over the fence for me." It's my old ball . . . my favorite! And you brought it to me. Thank you, thank you, Mrs. Bea! Of course I forgive you.

(*TEE hugs MRS. BEA.*)

TEE:     I'd like to say a little prayer, if it's okay.

(*TEE is still hugging MRS. BEA as he prays.*)

**Have Tee pray this prayer with the children:**
Dear God, bless our friends old and new. Help us love you . . . and love one another. Amen.

# WHAT IS ALL THIS HOOPLA?

<u>Characters:</u>
Mrs. Bea
Rev. Puggins


LEADER:     A revival had been planned months before, and last Sunday Rev. Puggins announced it during his service. Most folks were excited.

(*MRS. BEA is thinking out loud.*)

MRS. BEA:     Boy, I did some serious praying last week. I just prayed and prayed and prayed.

(*REV. PUGGINS comes on stage.*)

MRS. BEA:     Boy, did I ever pray. I never prayed so much in my life.

REV. PUGGINS:     Ummm . . . excuse me, Mrs. Bea, but I overheard you talking about all that praying. Were you helping us pray for the revival?

MRS. BEA:     Not exactly. I was praying more for . . . survival than revival. You see, I had to go across town. And our youth leader was driving; I needed lots of prayer!

REV. PUGGINS:     But you have been praying for the revival?

| | |
|---|---|
| MRS. BEA: | Ummm, not exactly. I'm not sure it needs me or my prayers! |
| REV. PUGGINS: | Oh, but it does! And if our revival doesn't have a foundation of prayer, it won't bring the changes we might need in our church, and ourselves! |
| MRS. BEA: | I don't think we need any changes here. So why bring somebody in here to stir things up? I like things just as they are! Besides, I have never met that preacher. |
| REV. PUGGINS: | We aren't just bringing in somebody! We invited a special preacher, and he/she has a wonderful way of sharing the Gospel. And anytime the Gospel is heard, hearts are warmed, and lives are changed. |
| MRS. BEA: | Do I have to change? If I have to change, count me out! |
| REV. PUGGINS: | No, you don't have to change. And you don't have to pray; and gosh, you don't even have to attend! But you'll be missing something. |
| MRS. BEA: | What? |
| REV. PUGGINS: | Well, let's see . . . you'll miss being with the people in our church; you'll miss the singing and prayers, and you'll miss hearing the special messages our guest pastor has for us. And you might just miss giving God a chance to make you one of his own special children. And believe it or not, we'd miss you! |

| | |
|---|---|
| MRS. BEA: | Well . . . ummm . . . I guess I'll try it out. But I think I'll sit in the back row. That is one of our traditions, isn't it? |
| REV. PUGGINS: | I'm afraid it is. I'll be looking for you tonight. But why don't we pray for all the folks and our revival now? I'd like the kids to help out. Okay? |
| MRS. BEA: | I suppose that would be okay. |

**Have Rev. Puggins pray this prayer with the children:**
Dear God, I want to pray for our guest preacher and for our revival, and I would also pray for all the folks who attend, especially those who sit on the back row. Bless each one. Amen.

# I'M ALMOST CONVINCED!

### Characters:
Mrs. Bea
Mrs. Munk

**LEADER:** Mrs. Bea came to the revival. True to her word, she sat on the back row. But Mrs. Bea is not a very large person, and she got really upset when someone almost sat on her on Tuesday night. Soon after the revival, she went hunting for Mrs. Munk.

**MRS. BEA:** Oh, Mrs. Munk . . . Are you home, Mrs. Munk? Can you come out for a moment?

(*MRS. MUNK comes on stage.*)

**MRS. MUNK:** Why, good morning, Mrs. Bea! Isn't this just a glorious day? And even if the weather isn't perfect, it's still just a wonderful day!

**MRS. BEA:** Ummm . . . why is that, Mrs. Munk?

**MRS. MUNK:** I guess I'm still flying pretty high, Mrs. Bea . . . you know, from the revival!

**MRS. BEA:** Yes, I sure do know. That's why I came to see you, Mrs. Munk.

**MRS. MUNK:** Oh, didn't you enjoy the revival? I thought the pastor was very special. I thought his/her preaching was really powerful.

**MRS. BEA:** I couldn't agree more, Mrs. Munk.

**MRS. MUNK:** Really? You thought it was . . . good?

**MRS. BEA:** I sure did. I have never heard anyone preach like that! He/she made God's Word so appetizing. Those sermons were like a fine steak dinner to a starving person! It was just something you couldn't resist! And I couldn't resist it, either!

**MRS. MUNK:** You mean something happened . . . to you?

**MRS. BEA:** Wow! Did it ever! I felt all this stuff inside. I felt like God really cared. I felt like I wasn't worthy. I felt like Jesus really died for me.

**MRS. MUNK:** And so you —

**MRS. BEA:** And so, I'm almost convinced. I'm almost ready to be baptized, almost ready to join the church.

**MRS. MUNK:** Almost? Is that all? That pastor poured out his heart, as well as showing us the heart of God . . . and you are *almost* convinced? You are *almost* ready to make a commitment and join the church?

**MRS. BEA:** Isn't it great? I think if I could hear a few more of those steak dinner sermons, I'd be ready to say yes to God!

**Mrs. Munk:** I don't want to disappoint you, Mrs. Bea, but he/she has gone back to his/her home church, and we are back to Rev. Puggins, our pastor and his beef stew sermons. I guess they aren't as exciting, but they are warm and pretty solid, as spiritual food goes.

**Mrs. Bea:** But I liked the way our guest pastor preached. It was so special. And boy, howdy, when he hit the pulpit with his hand . . . why, I got goose bumps all up my spine!

**Mrs. Munk:** I think he was planting some spiritual seeds among us. And now other preachers will be here to help the seeds grow. It takes lots of work, and sometimes the week-to-week work is not very exciting. But it is needed! So let's thank God for both the steak dinners and the beef stew preachers.

**Mrs. Bea:** Well, okay, if I can get some help . . . kids?

**Have Mrs. Bea pray this prayer with the children:**
Dear God, thank you for preachers who deliver your Word. Bless them all — big preachers, little preachers, steak preachers, and even beef stew preachers. Amen.

# A STRANGE FACE
# IN HARMONY

### Characters:
Mrs. Bea
Mrs. Munk
Tylertoo (see production notes)

### Production Notes:
*You will need a simple sock puppet.*

**LEADER:**    The revival service brought visitors to the
Harmony church. At least one of those folks
decided to come back. So now it's Sunday
morning . . . and on the back row of the
Harmony church, Mrs. Bea is whispering to Mrs.
Munk just before the church service begins.

**MRS. BEA:**    Ahem! Ahem! Mrs. Munk . . . Take a look over to
your right.

(*TYLERTOO, a sock puppet, is at far right. MRS. BEA and MRS.
MUNK turn to the right and stare.*)

**MRS. MUNK:**    Why I believe we have a visitor this morning,
Mrs. Bea!

(*MRS. MUNK turns toward the front.*)

**MRS. BEA:**    Dressed like that, must be a country music
singer! Why that hat . . . it's as bad as any I ever
saw! Never saw such . . . and in church too!

**149**

| | |
|---|---|
| **Mrs. Munk:** | I think it's a lovely hat. Why don't we go over and meet our visitor? |
| **Mrs. Bea:** | Uhhh, I don't think so. I'm not sure he is my kind of person. |
| **Mrs. Munk:** | Weren't you ever a visitor? |
| **Mrs. Bea:** | Well . . . umm . . . uhhh, yes, I guess I was, a few months ago. |
| **Mrs. Munk:** | And did members make you feel welcome to our church? |
| **Mrs. Bea:** | Let's see . . . you came right over. So did Grumpy, and Rev. Puggins, and Grandpa, and Tee too. |
| **Mrs. Munk:** | And how did that make you feel? |
| **Mrs. Bea:** | I felt like . . . ummm . . . like, uhhh, they wanted me to be there? I think. |
| **Mrs. Munk:** | They did want you to be there. That is why they are so friendly. Rev. Puggins is getting ready for the service. So we are the ones to say "welcome to the Harmony church!" It's not so hard . . . come on. |

(*Mrs. Munk and Mrs. Bea move over to the sock puppet.*)

| | |
|---|---|
| **Mrs. Munk:** | Hi there, I'm Mrs. Munk. And (*Motions to Mrs. Bea*) this is Mrs. Bea. We'd like to welcome you to the Harmony church. And if you aren't sitting with someone, we'd like for you to sit with us. |
| **Tylertoo:** | Hi! What a nice welcoming committee! My name is Tylertoo. |

| | |
|---|---|
| MRS. BEA: | Tylertoo . . . unusual name. Are you from Latagonia, maybe? |
| TYLERTOO: | I've never really heard of Latagonia. I've never been there. I wasn't even sure I wanted to come to here today . . . but you two make me glad that I did! I'm visiting kinfolk in this area . . . for a few more days. I'm a Christian too and wanted to try this church, especially after that revival! It was great! |
| MRS. MUNK: | Who are you visiting, Tylertoo? We might know them. |
| TYLERTOO: | I'm visiting a great couple. They just had a baby. I wanted to be on hand for that wonderful moment. I hoped that if it was a boy, they might name it Calvin. |
| MRS. BEA: | I think we know them . . . believe they go to church here! But are you sure about that name . . . Calvin? I think Bucky would have been a better name! I know at least six boys named Bucky. Yeah, Bucky! |
| MRS. MUNK: | Let's leave that up to the parents. Now let's thank God for the new folks who come into our lives . . . okay? |

**Have Mrs. Munk pray this prayer with the children:**
Dear God, thanks for the new folks who bless our lives — precious babies and visitors in church and neighbors who move in. Help us welcome them with love. Amen.

# TEE WANTS TO KNOW ABOUT HIS FRIENDS IN LOUISIANA

**Characters:**
Tee
Grandpa

**LEADER:**   The folks around Harmony held a celebration a couple of weeks ago. A terrible storm named Isidore had appeared off the coast, and all the citizens had looked for a place to hide. Mrs. Munk had gone down to the deepest part of her basement. Grumpy found a cave under a rock ledge; Grandpa and Tee went into a storm cellar. But Isidore didn't hit Harmony, and everyone was happy that his or her home was not destroyed. Everyone was happy until Tee saw in a newspaper that lots of people in Louisiana did lose their homes and their jobs and their cars . . . some even lost their lives. It was a terrible thing! Tee visited Grandpa with serious questions.

**TEE:**   Grandpa, does God love us more than God loves the people in Louisiana?

**GRANDPA:**   I'm sure not. Why do you ask, Tee?

**TEE:** Well . . . well, we thought that nasty storm named Isidore (*or the latest storm*) was going to hit us in Harmony, but it skipped right on by and hit Louisiana really hard. Does that mean God likes us, but doesn't like Louisiana? Are we better people than they are, or what? See, I have some friends back in Louisiana, and if God doesn't love them there, maybe they should all move to Harmony!

**GRANDPA:** I suppose there are places that are good or evil. Our Bible talks about some evil cities. But I don't think God hit Louisiana with a storm because it's an evil place! The Bible also tells us that rain falls on the just (or good) and the unjust (or bad) alike.

**TEE:** It really fell this time! Those folks needed an ark! It just rained and flooded everything. Now the water is full of germs, the crops are ruined, the cattle have drowned, and the homes are full of mud. Why it's even worse than the storm we had back last year!

**GRANDPA:** It sure is, Tee. We are already recovering. It'll be years before parts of Louisiana recover. It's really a sad thing! But lots of times the saddest things are just opportunities for God to do God's work. Churches find lots to do when there is trouble.

**TEE:** But what can we do? We are just a small church.

GRANDPA:   But we are also a small part of a big church. And the big church has been on the scene for a couple of weeks now, furnishing money, materials, and volunteers. It will help organize lots of people. It will take in food, clothing, drinking water, and maybe cleaning supplies.

TEE:   Gosh, how can I be a part of that?

GRANDPA:   You are already a part of it, Tee. A portion of every dollar you put in the offering goes to help people in trouble. It's just a part of being a church. But there is also a special fund to send even more help. If you have a spare dollar or two, you might write on it "disaster relief — Louisiana!"

TEE:   Well, I feel a little better about it. But could we also say a prayer for those people?

GRANDPA:   Sure, that's an important way to help. Boys and girls, please join us.

**Have Grandpa pray this prayer with the children:**
Dear God, we ask you to stay close to those who are suffering today. Give them courage and faith. Help them find new hope, and help us to help them. In Jesus' name, Amen.

# GRUMPY TELLS TEE ABOUT PLEDGE CARDS

### Characters:
Tee
Grumpy

**LEADER:** Tee picked up his mail at the Harmony post office and was a little bit surprised by a note that had a pledge card attached. The note came from the finance chairman of the Harmony church . . . It was asking Tee to think about what he was giving to the Lord. But Tee had some questions . . .

**TEE:** Hi, Grumpy, you are just the guy I wanted to see!

**GRUMPY:** Hi there, Tee. *Harumph!* What's up?

**TEE:** Ahhh, nothing much. Have you picked up your mail?

**GRUMPY:** Sure, I picked it up right after lunch. Why?

**TEE:** See anything strange in your mail?

**GRUMPY:** *Harumph!* Nope . . . Did you get something strange?

TEE: Well, I don't know! It might be strange. It's a note from the church asking me to think about what I will give next year.

GRUMPY: Oh yeah, I got that one, too. It's not so strange!

TEE: But I haven't ever done that before.

(*TEE starts speaking in a whiny or whimpering tone.*)

TEE: What if I can't make enough money to give what I say I'll give? Will God be really mad? Or will old Rev. Puggins kick me out of the church? See, I don't get much allowance.

GRUMPY: Nah, God won't be mad, and Rev. Puggins doesn't ever even see your pledge card. As far as money goes, you get lots more than I do, Tee. Last year at about this time — *Harumph!* — Grandpa explained this stuff to me. He said, "Just give what you can." And during this year I bet I have — *Harumph!* — given as much as I could . . . well, almost as much as I could! I'm not sure how my gifts are being used by the — *Harumph!* — church, but Rev. Puggins isn't losing any weight!

TEE: I bet he's giving some of your offering to that poor family just over the hill. I bet your gifts are helping other folks. And maybe that family will know a little more about Jesus because of you!

GRUMPY: *Harumph!* I hope so. But now that you — *Harumph!* — understand a little about our church, you think you can fill out your card?

TEE:            I think I can, Grumpy. I guess I can just fill it out
                in faith. But then what do I do?

GRUMPY:         Ask one of the kids to put it on the altar for you.
                That is where it belongs. For you are — *Harumph!*
                — giving it to God.

TEE:            Kids, would you join me?


**Have Tee pray this prayer with the children:**
Dear God, please bless our gifts. We don't have a whole lot of
money, but we want to share what we have with you. Use our
gifts to share your love with other people. Amen.

# GRUMPY ASKS REV. PUGGINS ABOUT THE MISSION IN AFRICA

### Characters:
Grumpy
Rev. Puggins

Substitute any mission activity your church is engaged in.

**LEADER:** One of the little kids — Grumpy calls them Munksters — made an appeal to the Harmony church for gifts to send on a mission venture. But the little Munkster didn't explain what it was all about, and Grumpy was suspicious.

**GRUMPY:** Hi, Rev. Puggins. *Harumph!* I'd like to ask a question, if you're not too busy thinking heavenly thoughts!

**REV. PUGGINS:** Grumpy, I'm afraid that my thoughts are not heavenly very often. I try to think heavenly thoughts, but sometimes I don't feel plugged into God. Now, what's your question?

**GRUMPY:** Oh, just this. *Harumph!* One of the Munksters asked for money to send for a school in Africa, and I just wondered why we should do that?

REV. PUGGINS: We do it because we are Christians, Grumpy. There are thousands of kids in Africa who have been made orphans by violence, terrorism, and war. They have no place to be, no place to grow, and no one to show them love. These schools will give them a chance at life.

GRUMPY: But — *Harumph!* — aren't those kids really different from us?.

REV. PUGGINS: What do you mean different, Grumpy?

(*REV. PUGGINS lifts his head to heaven.*)

GRUMPY: Well, they don't dress the way we do, and they sure don't wear their hair the way we do.

REV. PUGGINS: Grumpy, does the way we dress or the way we wear our hair really make any difference as to how we are as people, or how we are deserving of help? By the way, did you choose to look the way you look?

GRUMPY: I didn't choose. *Harumph!* I was born this way. Oh, I see what you mean. Nobody chooses the way they look or even the country they live in.

REV. PUGGINS: Yep, you are getting close to some heavenly thoughts now, Grumpy. God wants all God's people to live in harmony and peace. This mission effort for the African kids will help create just a little more harmony and peace in a troubled world. I hope you will donate. It might make a difference. But now, why don't you lead our kids here in a prayer for those African children?

GRUMPY:    Okay, but it seems like I've been praying a lot lately! Here goes . . . kids, are you — *Harumph!* — with me? Well, here goes . . .


**Have Grumpy pray this prayer with the children:**
Dear God, we ask your blessings on the kids of Africa. Help us do whatever we can do to show them your love — and our love. *Harumph!* Help us all live in peace and harmony. Amen.

# GRUMPY'S FUNNY HAT

### Characters:
Grumpy
Mrs. Munk

### Prop:
a tall pilgrim-type black hat

LEADER: Rev. Puggins was disappointed to discover that the young couple named their baby Ryan Joseph instead of Calvin. Mrs. Bea was devastated that they had not chosen Bucky. She thought it was such a nice name. She knows lots of boys named Bucky. Now a special Sunday has arrived, and Grumpy caught up with Mrs. Munk on the path to church.

(*GRUMPY is wearing a tall pilgrim-type black hat.*)

GRUMPY: Oh, hi, Mrs. Munk. How are you and all the little Munksters?

MRS. MUNK: The Munksters are just fine, but I have a headache this morning, Grumpy.

GRUMPY: I'd give you an aspirin, but . . . (*Giggle*) . . . I must have left them in my other coat.

MRS. MUNK: I'm not in the mood for jokes, Grumpy. Everybody knows you only have one coat, and you never seem to take it off! But speaking of headaches, what is that tall thing on your head? It looks a little like a hat and a little like a skyscraper. It sure is tall.

GRUMPY: I'll wear it in the school play on Wednesday, Mrs. Munk.

MRS. MUNK: Oh, it must be about those strange people from outer space . . . you know, the coneheads. I guess that hat would hide the cone all right!

GRUMPY: Did you forget, Mrs. Munk?

MRS. MUNK: Forget what?

GRUMPY: That Thursday is Thanksgiving Day. And on Wednesday we have a church play all about pilgrims, and Indians, and a big feast!

MRS. MUNK: Now I get it . . . you'll be a pilgrim, right?

GRUMPY: Not just a pilgrim. I'm going to be William Bradford, the first governor in Plymouth. I wanted to be Miles Standish and carry a musket, but Rev. Puggins picked out somebody else for that part.

MRS. MUNK: Will you have a speaking part?

GRUMPY: I only have one line, and it goes:

(*Grumpy does a John Wayne imitation.*)

GRUMPY: Walll, pillgrum! I say that same line at three different place. The preacher thinks it's funny. I'm not sure why. It's just this: "Walll, pillgrum, . . ."

MRS. MUNK: Sounded like John Wayne to me. (*Giggles*) You sure you've got on the right kind of hat?

GRUMPY: Oh, sure! And when the pilgrims give thanks, I get to be at the head of the table. They were famous for giving thanks, you know.

MRS. MUNK: Yes, I know that story. And I'd like to give thanks right now . . . okay, boys and girls?

**Have Mrs. Munk pray this prayer with the children:**
Dear God, thank you for the pilgrims, who taught us to be thankful. Thank you for our country. We pray that all people may some day live in peace and harmony. Amen.

# MRS. BEA: WHY SHOULD I GIVE THANKS?

### Characters:
Mrs. Bea
Mrs. Munk

**LEADER:** Autumn seems to have slipped into the village as quietly as a falling leaf. Some of the residents are surprised that Thanksgiving will soon arrive. Their plans are incomplete. But one resident doesn't seem to be preparing.

**MRS. BEA:** Oh, Mrs. Munk! Yoo hoo, Mrs. Munk! Are you there?

(*MRS. MUNK comes up to the stage.*)

**MRS. MUNK:** Yes, I'm home; I was just working on my guest list for the big Thanksgiving dinner. I hope you can be with us. We'd love for you to join us . . . and oh, it's a covered dish thing; so bring your favorite dish.

**MRS. BEA:** Don't see much sense in it, myself.

**MRS. MUNK:** Whaaat?

**MRS. BEA:** I said, I don't see much sense in it . . . all that Thanksgiving stuff!

| | |
|---|---|
| MRS. MUNK: | But . . . but, Mrs. Bea, it's such a nice holiday. |
| MRS. BEA: | Not for somebody whose home got washed away in the flood last year, it isn't! |
| MRS. MUNK: | Yeah, I guess you have had some troubles. |
| MRS. BEA: | Some troubles? I've had a whole wagonload! |
| MRS. MUNK: | I guess so. But now Grandpa was pretty sick for a while. Remember when he went to that clinic? And the guy has had to move twice, which is never fun. And Tee wrecked his car when he hit that stump. And before all that, his barn burned down! I'd say Grandpa has had a lot more troubles than you have. |
| MRS. BEA: | So what? |
| MRS. MUNK: | So I've asked Grandpa to say the Thanksgiving prayer when we have this covered dish dinner. He was delighted that I asked him! He's already started thinking about the ways God has blessed his life. |
| MRS. BEA: | Oh. |
| MRS. MUNK: | I do hope you'll join us. We'll save a seat for you. And by your plate I'll put five grains of dried corn. |
| MRS. BEA: | I don't think dried corn is on my diet. Sounds pretty strange to me. |

| | |
|---|---|
| MRS. MUNK: | Those five kernels of corn are just a reminder . . . something the pilgrims used to do long ago . . . reminded them of those days when five grains of corn was all they had for a whole day, and even with just five grains, they gave thanks! |
| MRS. BEA: | Oh. So you're telling me that all these people give thanks even when their lives are really dark and it looks like there's no light at the end of the tunnel? |
| MRS. MUNK: | Absolutely! And it would do you good to look for blessings in life, instead of the darkness! |
| MRS. BEA: | You really think so? Well, I might show up. I can always use a good meal. |
| MRS. MUNK: | We'll have a place for you. But right now, I'd like to offer a little Thanksgiving prayer. You see, Grandpa and I talked about this last week. Help out, kids! |

**Have Mrs. Munk pray this prayer with the children:**
Dear God, for parents, for our church, for friends, for homes, for good food, and for all our other blessings, we give you thanks. Amen.

# DECISIONS, DECISIONS, DECISIONS!

### Characters:
Mrs. Bea
Mrs. Munk


**LEADER:** Grumpy wore his funny hat in the church play and was quite a hit when he said, "Waalll, pillgrum,"—his only line. A couple of days later, Mrs. Munk was napping — still full of Thanksgiving food — when Mrs. Bea came knocking.

(*MRS. BEA goes upstairs to the stage. She looks all around. Tap the microphone a few times to make a knocking sound as she knocks on the door. Pause. Tap the microphone again.*)

**MRS. BEA:** Yoo hoo, Mrs. Munk. It's me, Mrs. Bea.

(*Mrs. Munk appears to climb upstairs to the stage. She yawns and stretches.*)

**MRS. MUNK:** Oh, hi, Mrs. Bea.

**MRS. BEA:** Hi, Mrs. Munk. Glad I caught you at home.

**MRS. MUNK:** Ummm . . . yes. I had just put the Munksters down for a nap and was "resting my eyes. "

**MRS. BEA:** I rest my eyes sometimes. I think I snore when I rest my eyes.

MRS. MUNK: I probably snore too! What brings you to my house today, Mrs. Bea?

MRS. BEA: It's all this business about decisions. I was almost convinced to become — you know — a Christian . . . back when we had the revival, but I'm just not real good at making important decisions like that. You know what I mean?

MRS. MUNK: Not exactly. We make important decisions all the time.

MRS. BEA: What do you mean?

MRS. MUNK: Well, let's see. You decided when to get up this morning, what to have for breakfast, which apron to wear, you decided you needed to talk to someone, . . . and you decided to come and see me. The only thing you really didn't decide on was whether to breathe or not. I think that is automatic.

MRS. BEA: But those decisions weren't that important, were they?

MRS. MUNK: Well, they could be, because our small decisions can help us with the larger decisions. Your decision to come here today might help you understand something important.

MRS. BEA: So I'm making important decisions . . . every day?

| | |
|---|---|
| MRS. MUNK: | That's right. But real decisions call for real commitment. Maybe it is commitment you are having trouble with, instead of decisions. God calls us to make a solid commitment . . . but the world is always trying to pull us away. |
| MRS. BEA: | So a decision by itself isn't enough? |
| MRS. MUNK: | A decision for anything — a job, a spouse, a business deal, or faith — without commitment is empty. It's like a big balloon . . . looks nice and solid until it runs into trouble . . . then, bang! It's gone! |
| MRS. BEA: | Oh dear! I thought I had put this all together. Now you talk about commitment, and I have to go back and think some more. |
| MRS. MUNK: | I hope you'll pray while you think. That's an important decision we make too. And if the boys and girls will help, we'll ask God to be our guide. |

**Have Mrs. Munk pray this prayer with the children:**
Dear God, help us make the right decisions every day of our lives. And help us have the commitment we need to put you in the center of our lives. Amen.

# HARMONY AND THE ELECTION

### Characters:
Mrs. Bea
Mrs. Munk


**LEADER:** There is quite a buzz going on in Harmony. It seems that the number of people who voted for the leaders of the country might just decide who wins. There has been talk about recounts and court appeals . . . and all sorts of things. Mrs. Munk and Mrs. Bea aren't sure what is going to happen, but that doesn't stop them from talking about it!

**MRS. BEA:** Fancy meeting you here at Petunia's Hair Salon, Mrs. Munk. I didn't know you indulged in this sort of thing.

**MRS. MUNK:** I'm only here to get my nails done, Mrs. Bea. Digging in the flower bed really messes up my nails!

**MRS. BEA:** Ummm, yes, I suppose so . . . never enjoyed digging, myself. Oh . . . uh . . . being residents of Harmony, how do you think we should vote? After all, our votes might determine who wins!

**MRS. MUNK:** Well, Mrs. Bea, I've given a lot of thought to this . . . and I really think we should cast our votes for the one who enjoys gardening. It just seems fair to me that way!

**MRS. BEA:** I'm not sure I agree! I think the candidates who eat only vegetables and fruit will get my vote.!

**MRS. MUNK:** And the one who can tell good stories. Now, that's a real gift. We should give our votes to the one who is the best storyteller!

**MRS. BEA:** Well, I really think we should cast our ballots for the one who can swim best . . . or an athlete! He'd be a real winner!

**MRS. MUNK:** I don't think swimming is all that important, Mrs. Bea!

**MRS. BEA:** Well, neither is storytelling. Who ever heard of such?

**MRS. MUNK:** Does this mean we don't agree on who should be leader?

**MRS. BEA:** Exactly! We may take awhile to decide which candidate is the best one for the job. And the job won't be easy, no matter who gets it!

**MRS. MUNK:** You can say that again!

**MRS. BEA:** The job won't be —

MRS. MUNK: (*Interrupts*) And because the job won't be easy, let's have a prayer for whoever wins, okay, boys and girls? Would you pray with me for our leaders?

**Have Mrs. Munk pray this prayer with the children:**
Dear God, we trust you to help us pick the right man or woman to be our leader, even if that person can't swim or doesn't like gardening. We know you will be there with him or her, leading him or her toward right decisions. Guide and protect our elected leaders and give them your blessings. Amen.

# HARMONY PRAYS FOR OUR ELECTED LEADERS

### Characters:
Grandpa
Mrs. Munk

| | |
|---|---|
| **LEADER:** | Let's listen in today as Grandpa helps Mrs. Munk understand something about being a good citizen. |
| **GRANDPA:** | Oh, hi there, Mrs. Munk. Did you watch the election returns? |
| **MRS. MUNK:** | Heavens, no! I don't like those things! |
| **GRANDPA:** | You mean our leaders? You don't like our elected leaders? |
| **MRS. MUNK:** | No, I don't! Didn't vote for them . . . won't watch them sworn into office . . . got burned out with the whole election mess! |
| **GRANDPA:** | Gosh, that's too bad. Didn't know you were old enough to vote, though. |
| **MRS. MUNK:** | I'm thirty something, just like the TV show! And I'm certainly old enough to vote. |

GRANDPA: Umm . . . Oh yes, we were talking about the election. I was just about to say a prayer for our elected leaders. This is a really tough time in our history. I think they would like to know people are praying for them. Would you join me, Mrs. Munk . . . boys and girls?

MRS. MUNK: Why? Didn't vote for them . . . don't like them!

GRANDPA: Ulp . . . umm . . . er . . . Well, they are our leaders, and they do not have easy jobs. They need both our prayers and support to do a good job. Anyone who moves into a high office needs God's blessings and needs God's help. At least, that's what I think.

MRS. MUNK: Well, okay. I guess one little prayer won't hurt me and might do them some good!

GRANDPA: Okay, let's bow our heads then.

**Have Grandpa pray this prayer with the children:**
Dear God, we ask you to give our elected officials (MRS. MUNK *looks over at* GRANDPA) . . . wisdom and compassion. Enable them to do great things for this country and your kingdom. Amen.

GRANDPA: Say "Amen," Mrs. Munk.

MRS. MUNK: Okay. Amen!

# MRS. BEA
# WANTS TO KNOW
# ABOUT ADVENT

### Characters:
Mrs. Bea
Grandpa

**LEADER:** At the Harmony church service last week, Mrs. Munk and her little Munksters lit the second Advent candle. Throughout the service Mrs. Bea looked puzzled. After the service ended, Mrs. Bea caught up with Grandpa on the path.

**MRS. BEA:** Oh, Grandpa! Wait up, Grandpa! Don't walk so fast.

**GRANDPA:** Oh, hi, Mrs. Bea. That's the first time anyone accused me of walking fast in . . . oh gosh, maybe thirty years.

**MRS. BEA:** I guess your legs are a lot longer. Maybe you just take bigger steps!

**GRANDPA:** I guess that's it, Mrs. Bea. Wasn't our service nice today? And the little Munksters did a fine job with the Advent wreath, didn't they?

| | |
|---|---|
| MRS. BEA: | I guess so, Grandpa. That's why I stopped you. It looked to me like they didn't light all the candles, and I'm not sure what an Advent wreath is, anyway! I thought wreaths were hung on the door. That one is laying flat . . . doesn't make good sense to me. |
| GRANDPA: | This wreath is very special, Mrs Bea. It lays flat so it can be the base for five special candles. Each candle in that wreath has a special meaning. Last week was the prophet's candle, and this week we'll light the candle of love. |
| MRS. BEA: | I remember something about prophecy . . . one of the Munksters read from Isaiah, I think. |
| GRANDPA: | That's right. Each candle helps us remember how much the world needed Jesus and how we get ready for his arrival. Then, on Christmas Eve, we light the one center candle, and it represents Jesus' birth. |
| MRS. BEA: | Then Advent must mean something like . . . uhhh . . . uhhh . . . |
| GRANDPA: | The coming . . . the coming of Christ to a world that needs him so badly. And as we light the candles of Advent, we prepare in our hearts a place for him. Is there a place for him in your heart, Mrs. Bea? |
| MRS. BEA: | Why, . . . uh . . . yes. I think so. But I thought he just needed a stable and a box of straw. Isn't that enough? |

| | |
|---|---|
| GRANDPA: | That was enough on that night when he was born, but he also needs to be born in each one of our hearts — if there is room in there for him. |
| MRS. BEA: | Well, let's just imagine that, maybe . . . uh, just maybe there isn't a place in my . . . uh, somebody's heart, how does that person make a place for him, Grandpa? |
| GRANDPA: | I would guess that you'd have to get rid of stuff that was crowding him out. Some folks might say we need to carry out the trash, especially the mean or hateful stuff. Another way is to pray that God will make a place in our hearts for the Savior. Would you like to do that, Mrs. Bea? |
| MRS. BEA: | Well, yes, of course, if my friends will help. Will you, boys and girls? |
| GRANDPA: | OK, let us pray. |

**Have Grandpa pray this prayer with the children:**
Dear God, help us get ready for the birth of Jesus in our hearts, and in our world. Help me take the trash out of my life so he will have a clean place. Amen.

# MRS. BEA
# WANTS TO KNOW
# ABOUT ANGELS

### Characters:
Mrs. Bea
Rev. Puggins


**LEADER:** After a pretty quiet week, there was a bit of excitement in Harmony. It happened one afternoon when Mrs. Bea showed up at Rev. Puggins' home. She was pretty excited . . . but we'll let her tell what happened . . .

**MRS. BEA:** Rev. Puggins! Oh, Rev. Puggins! Wake up, Rev. Puggins!

(*REV. PUGGINS jerks his head up abruptly.*)

**REV. PUGGINS:** Oh! Uhhh, hi there, Mrs. Bea. You caught me in the midst of my afternoon siesta.

**MRS. BEA:** Looked like you were just taking a nap, to me. But never mind. I've got a very important question for you.

**REV. PUGGINS:** What's that, Mrs. Bea?

| | |
|---|---|
| MRS. BEA: | What do angels look like, Rev. Puggins? Could they look like you or me? Do they look like . . . say, somebody in the choir? Or are they different? |
| REV. PUGGINS: | Why the sudden interest in angels, Mrs. Bea? |
| MRS. BEA: | I think I've seen one! I had a flat tire a few days ago, and I didn't know how to change it. It was nighttime, and I was scared. |
| REV. PUGGINS: | Sounds like you were in big, big trouble! |
| MRS. BEA: | Oh, I was in very big trouble! But that night something really strange happened. |
| REV. PUGGINS: | Strange? |
| MRS. BEA: | Very strange! I was ready to spend the night in that car when a fellow showed up and asked if he could help. I was scared at first. But he seemed nice, so I let him get the spare out of the trunk. Then he changed the tire. I offered him money, a new five-dollar bill, but he said, "No thanks, just try to help someone else sometime." |
| REV. PUGGINS: | I suppose angels could look like whatever God wants them to look like. And sometimes our angels are really just people doing angelic work. In both cases we should remember the psalm that says, "Where does my help come from? My help comes from the Lord." |
| MRS. BEA: | I guess that makes sense. So I should thank God for angels, whatever they look like? |

REV. PUGGINS:   Sure.

MRS. BEA:   And could I ask God to help my old car keep going? I really need it.

REV. PUGGINS:   Sure, why not?

MRS. BEA:   Boys and girls, let's talk to God.

**Have Mrs. Bea pray this prayer with the children:**
Dear God, thank you for angels, even if they look just like our friends. Help us with the things we need to make our lives easier. Amen.

# GRANDPA AND GRUMPY AT CHRISTMAS

**Characters:**
Grandpa
Grumpy

**LEADER:** A week or so ago, Grandpa got one of those nasty viruses that seem to be going around. He's a little weak now, but his spirits are high. Today he meets Grumpy at the entrance to the shopping mall.

**GRANDPA:** (*Cough, cough*) Why, hello, Grumpy. It's so good to see you again.

**GRUMPY:** Hi Grandpa. *Harumph!* Gosh, I've missed you around here.

**GRANDPA:** And you don't know how much I've missed being here. I missed watching folks decorate their homes, and I've almost missed my chance to do a little shopping for Christmas. In fact, for awhile there, I figured I'd seen my last Christmas tree.

**GRUMPY:** *Harumph!* You do look a little washed out.

**GRANDPA:** Washed out? I thought I was washed up!

| GRUMPY: | Oh, Grandpa, you'll be here for lots more Christmases! By the way, did I tell you that I showed up to try out for the cantata? Our choir leader said they weren't quite ready for someone with my talent. *Harumph!* I suppose they aren't quite up to my level of performance. I thought giving my talent would be a nice Christmas gift to the baby Jesus. I'm in one of those "fixed income situations," and now I don't know what I can give at Christmas. |
|---|---|
| GRANDPA: | (*Cough*) I don't think the shepherds had much to give Jesus, Grumpy. But as poor as they were, the angels selected them to be the very first guests at that wonderful birthday party. (*Cough*) Now, if they didn't have money to give, what do you think they gave the baby? |
| GRUMPY: | *Harumph!* Ummm . . . Uhhh . . . ummm, I guess they gave the baby Jesus their devotion, and maybe their admiration, and I guess their respect too. |
| GRANDPA: | Devotion, admiration, and respect; I think you could sum it all up with just one word, Grumpy. The shepherds welcomed Jesus into the world with their love. |
| GRUMPY: | I'd never — *Harumph!* — thought about it like that. But I guess love is the greatest gift we can give another person. |
| GRANDPA: | Do you think Jesus would like us to give him our love? |

GRUMPY: Makes sense to me, Grandpa! I'm glad you helped me out with this. I do love Jesus, Grandpa, and I love you . . . and shucks, I even love these boys and girls. But (*Mumbles*) I still might chase them out of my yard with a broom.

GRANDPA: What's that, Grumpy?

GRUMPY: Oh, nothing. I think it's probably time for us to ask our pastor to help us with a special Christmas prayer. Boys and girls, will you help too?

**Say a prayer with the children.**

# INDEX